HOW TO SURVIVE
ANYWHERE

D0681181

OTHER BOOKS BY CHRISTOPHER NYERGES

Extreme Simplicity: Homesteading in the City
(with Dolores Lynn Nyerges)

Guide to Wild Foods and Useful Plants

Enter the Forest

Testing Your Outdoor Survival Skills

Urban Wilderness: A Guidebook to Resourceful City Living

Wild Greens and Salads: A Cookbook

Guide to Wild Foods

HOW TO SURVIVE
ANYWHERE

*A Guide for Urban, Suburban, Rural,
and Wilderness Environments*

CHRISTOPHER NYERGES

STACKPOLE
BOOKS

Published by
STACKPOLE BOOKS
5067 Ritter Road
Mechanicsburg, PA 17055
www.stackpolebooks.com

Printed in the United States of America

10 9 8 7 6 5 4

First edition

Cover photograph of fire © Corbis
Cover design by Caroline Stover
Photographs by the author unless otherwise indicated

Library of Congress Cataloging-in-Publication Data

Nyerges, Christopher.
  How to survive anywhere / Christopher Nyerges.— 1st ed.
    p. cm.
  ISBN-10: 0-8117-3304-1
  ISBN-13: 978-0-8117-3304-5
  1. Survival skills. I. Title

  GF86.N84 2006
  613.6'9—dc22

                                                    2006000781

Contents

Foreword

by Ed Begley, Jr.

There is a widely held belief that the nature is somewhere "out there." That, when we speak of the environment, we're speaking about Yosemite or Yellowstone and certainly not talking about a city like Los Angeles or New York.

Christopher Nyerges shows us that the natural environment is all around us, wherever we live. And that we can soon master the skills that we need to better understand it, and even more importantly, to survive nearly anything that nature **OR** civilization can throw at us.

He also shows us that it's not just the environment that benefits from a path of greater simplicity. He points out that the rewards of this life style/mindset have less to do with a number on a bank statement and more to do with the number of hours spent in enjoyment with your family.

So, enjoy!

Introduction

Survival. What is *survival?* In the narrowest sense, it is simply the ability to resist all the forces of nature that seem to conspire to end or shorten our life. In one sense, survival is a relative concept, since the very nature of life on earth means that everything dies.

Survival means different things to different people. To a wilderness explorer, it means having the skills to stay alive for a night—or much longer—using only what nature has provided. To an urban dweller, it means having the wit and wisdom to protect yourself and your family from all the predators that seek to end or shorten your life. These can be of the human sort (terrorists, burglars, hijackers, scam artists, rapists) or they can be of the natural sort (earthquakes, hurricanes, floods, fires, drought).

We will address the basic skills needed to keep you alive and healthy in the woods and in the city. We will address these skills so you can be prepared, so you can act appropriately after a disaster strikes, and so that you can hopefully avoid a life-threatening survival situation in the first place.

In this book, we are not particularly interested in the very specific details of how to deal with a narrowly specific disaster. That has already been addressed in worst-case scenario type books.

We will focus upon the basics in the primary areas of concern: fire, water, food, shelter, clothing, tools and weapons, and more. In most cases, the skills and methods we describe can be practiced in either the city or the woods. Keep in mind that in severe urban disasters—such as Hurricane Katrina that wiped parts of cities right off the landscape—"urban survival" and "wilderness survival" became one and the same.

Additonally, we will go a bit further in this book. We will—in the last chapter—attempt to identify those behaviors and choices that inevitably lead us into life-threatening survival situations. We will provide real solutions that you can apply in your own life, in the wilderness or a rural setting, or in the city.

"Survival" is at least two things. First, it refers to those basic skills—purifying water, making fire, identifying plants—that can be applied by anyone, anywhere, under most circumstances. Those are the basics of individual security and survival. Second, survival also refers to the identification of those practices and principles that we can practice in our daily lives to enhance our survival and lead to full and productive lives. By necessity, this second aspect of survival leads us into the realms of economics, sociology, human relations, politics, and, yes, philosophy, religion, and spirituality.

Survival—in its fullest sense—is our most basic instinct. It is not merely a topic for a junior college adult education course. It is a way of life, a way of thinking, a way of living that enhances everything you do, and prepares you for whatever the uncertainties of life may bring. True survival is not narrowly selfish, greedy, racist, or hateful. Following this "counterfeit survival" is ultimately counterproductive to our individual and group survival. Real survival is expansive, giving, inclusive, and loving. It is this latter real survival that I hope to pass along. Please join me in this adventure.

1

Water

WATER EVERYWHERE—BUT IS IT SAFE TO DRINK?

Water is an extremely complex element. There was a time when I had a full file drawer of test data from water purification device manufacturers, all supposedly written by scientists, and all full of contradictory data. Unfortunately, each manufacturer of a water purification device had its own paid scientists to prove that its product was the best.

But I was constantly seeking the bottom line. What product *is*, objectively, "the best?" It wasn't an easy answer to find. In part, this is because of water's enormous complexity and the various components that contaminate water under different circumstances.

Plus, to the best of my knowledge, no company, agency, or government had ever taken all the water purification devices and tested them all with control water that contained measurable amounts of known pathogens. Such a test would not only be time-consuming and expensive but would still perhaps leave many questions unanswered.

I was eager to read about a field test that *Backpacker* magazine had conducted of several top water purification devices. This was not a test, however, of how well the devices actually purified water, but rather how easy the devices were to use in the field. It was an interesting test, but close to meaningless from my perspective.

As far as water purification devices are concerned, I'd concluded that the Katadyne products were the best you could buy—the Cadillac of water purification devices. They are generally the most expensive, they meet all federal guidelines, and they are typically carried into the field by Red Cross emergency workers under "primitive" conditions. Yet, spending the most isn't necessary, since nearly all water purification products meet the same federal guidelines.

In my classes where I taught (among other things) how to purify water in the wilderness and in the aftermath of an earthquake, I had to settle upon some basic advice that would be reliable in most situations.

Even though there are countless variables, here is the twenty-five-cent version of water purification that I have taught my students for nearly thirty years:

WATER PURIFICATION 101

- Distillation is the only absolute method of purification.
- Boiling kills everything that can make us sick, so it's the best field method of purification.
- If you can't boil, all the commercial filters that meet the federal guidelines of blocking everything larger than .02 microns are fine.
- Two of the halogen class of chemicals (chlorine and iodine) can be used, but each has its pros and cons. Tincture of iodine, for example, has a shelf life of about two years. But if you have iodine crystals in a glass jar with a bit of water, the solution will be viable as long as there are crystals in the water.
- Household bleach (2 percent chlorine) is ineffective with seriously polluted water. It is useful for retarding the growth of algae in water you intend to store, however.

That's the outline of *Water Purification 101*, how to purify water in a nutshell. But there is so much more to the subject! Even some of what I thought was true in my twenty-five-cent synopsis *is not!*

LET'S TAKE A CLOSER LOOK AT WATER

Richard Redman teaches ecology, environmental science, chemistry, and biology at Franklin High School in the hilly Highland Park district of Los Angeles.

On an early Saturday morning, I spotted him with a dozen of his students along the foggy wet banks of Southern California's Arroyo Seco, showing them how to test and measure water quality.

He paused to explain to me the seven measurements his students would be taking at different locations.

First, he says, the students measure the amount of dissolved oxygen in the water. He pointed out that when water gets colder, there's more oxygen dissolved into the water. This is critical for aquatic life.

Next, they test for the presence of nitrogen, which comes naturally from dissolving rocks and minerals, and wild animal waste. The students also test for phosphates.

Redman points out that both nitrogen and phosphates can come from pollutants, but they can also come from natural sources. Both of these are fertilizers and support plant growth. "About 4 ppm [parts per million] is the normal amount of nitrogen and phosphates to be found in water in this area. But when golf courses and farming areas put these fertilizers into their soil, they will leach out into the water table and increase the concentrates of both in the water. Higher concentrates of nitrogen and phosphates cause algae blooms. As these algae grow and then die, the decomposing algae use the dissolved oxygen in the water, and this can have a dramatic effect on the fish and other aquatic life."

Redman's students also do a pH test, which determines the acid-to-alkaline level of the water. For example, most of the particulate matter in the air of Southern California comes from diesel vehicles. "These hydrocarbons eventually get into the water chain, typically from rain washing them into the ground and rivers," says Redman. A pH test does not, however, determine a source of pollution, per se. It merely tells the acid/alkaline level. Acid rain, for example, associated with the environment of the northeastern United States, is caused by factory emissions and vehicle emissions. He adds that, "We don't really have acid rain in California."

The students then test the water for turbidity. This is a visual check of the water to determine its relative clarity. High turbidity is caused by microorganisms and mostly sediment in the water. His students also record water temperatures.

Determining the volume of water going downstream is also done. Redman has his students note how the nitrogen and phosphate levels in the same stream will change as the volume of water changes. "In the winter when there is typically a greater volume of water, the nitrogen and phosphates are diluted," he explains.

Redman's students are learning about the ecology of water, and how each factor of water quality can affect another factor. "By taking seven different measurements, my students are learning that there is a whole chain of events that takes place when you do things to water. For example, trout like a maximum temperature of twenty-two degrees Celsius, or seventy-two degrees Fahrenheit. But if the temperature of the water goes up—and this can occur naturally or as a result of run-off or water discharged from some industrial source—the dissolved oxygen count in the water goes down. Less

Richard Redman records the air temperature as a part of his testing procedure.

Richard Redman takes a water sample for a nitrogen test.

Comparing colors with a water sample to determine the level of nitrogen in the water.

oxygen in the water means less trout, as well as other reduced aquatic life," says Redman.

How does all this relate to testing water for potability? Most biologists and hydrologists agree that there is no way you can determine whether or not water is safe to drink simply by looking at it.

Some of the tests that Redman teaches his students are useful for determining relative water safety. For example, if the pH test shows highly acidic water, you could have contamination from a natural or man-made cause. High levels of nitrogen could indicate runoff from a local golf course, or possibly something natural.

But for the average person, backpacking in a wilderness area, or in need of water after a major earthquake or tsunami, how can you decide which water to drink, and how to purify the water if needed?

Most health and wilderness experts worldwide say you should always assume that open water sources are unsafe to drink, unless you find out otherwise. This very conservative viewpoint does not mean that all open sources of water are polluted; it's simply solid advice to avoid getting extremely sick from bad water. In most areas, water is tested by hydrologists or biologists, and if you do your homework before you enter a new wilderness area, you'll have good information about the water's purity.

Even when the water in an area is believed to be pure, it's important to use common sense. Redman points out that there are many ways in which a local area of an otherwise pure stream can be polluted. "Make sure there's no dead animal upstream, and always be observant for sloppy campers." In some heavily used campgrounds, lazy or ignorant campers toss garbage, baby diapers, and old food into the stream.

OK, so the water's polluted. How do we purify it?

PURIFICATION

Boiling is generally considered the best way to purify water from biological contaminants. Nearly every water expert I spoke with agreed on this point.

Antoni van Leeuwenhoek (1632–1723) discovered that some organisms do survive boiling. Fortunately, the majority of organisms that cause sickness in humans are killed by boiling. It turns out, however, that typhoid spores survive boiling. Normally, you'll only encounter typhoid in the water after a hurricane, or major earthquake, where sewage water mixes with the drinking water. Though somewhat rare today, it's still possible to get typhoid spores in open sources of water that would survive boiling.

So how long would it take to actually kill those spores? This has to do with such factors as temperature, exposure to sunlight, the amount of spores in the water, whether or not you did any of the primary or secondary levels of purification, and so on. In areas with heavily polluted water, up to twenty minutes may be required to break down those spore casings, and the water would then be safe to drink. Even if you consumed some, they do degrade with time. Whether you get sick or not depends on your state of health.

When water is suspected of being impure, experts suggests a three-step process of purification.

First, filter open sources of water through something like cotton to remove all larger particulate matter.

Second, let the water settle, and siphon out the clear water.

Third, boil. If you cannot boil, use chemicals.

CHEMICALS

Two of the halogen class of chemicals—chlorine and iodine—can be used to kill biological organisms in water. Each has its own pros and cons. *(Fluorine, also in this class of chemicals, is often added to city water supplies—but not for water purification.)*

Chlorine

Though chlorine is the stronger and more reactive of the two (chlorine and iodine), it is commonly available in households in the form of bleach, a solution of 2 percent chlorine. Though long suggested as a water purification method, the addition of a few drops of household bleach to suspect water is viable only in cases of the less-polluted water. It is not viable for heavily polluted water; the amount of bleach that must be added to assure "purity" renders the water unpalatable.

More convenient is a pill manufactured by Continental Technologies (255 Main St., P.O. Box 128, Little River, KS 67457) called Redi Chlor. The active ingredient is calcium hypochlorite (70 percent), with a minimum available chlorine of 70 percent. You add one pill to two gallons.

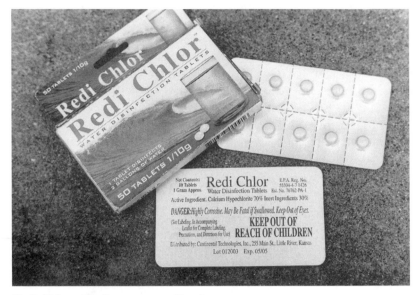

Redi Chlor pills for water purification.

There is a shelf life of a few years, and the expiration is printed on the package. Clearly labeled as highly corrosive, the pills are possibly fatal if swallowed whole.

Iodine

As for iodine, the best iodine method of purifying water is with the crystals. Iodine crystals, however, have been harder and harder to obtain for legitimate uses because illegal drug manufacturers use them for making methamphetamines. Assuming you can find some (or find a source of the premade water purification kits), here is how you do it.

Put about one-quarter teaspoon of the iodine crystals (USP grade, resublimated iodine) into a one-ounce glass jar with a hard-plastic lid. Typically, the lid is a measuring device. Add water to the bottle, and when the water is at body temperature, the water will turn a golden color. Pour 10cc of the golden water into a quart of suspect water. Wait from five to ten minutes before drinking. Longer times are required in colder temperatures.

A 5cc cap requires two capfuls of the golden liquid to purify a quart of water; a 10cc cap requires only one capful of the liquid for a quart of suspect water.

At left, a one-ounce glass jar with iodine crystals inside. In the middle, a small amount of iodine crystals. At right, iodine crystals with water added.

Pouring a cupful (10cc) of the saturated iodine solution into a quart of suspect water. DUDE McLEAN

Once you have used up the golden liquid in the bottle, simply continue to add water. As long as you have crystals, this golden liquid is viable as a water purifier. The shelf life of the crystals can last into years.

Tincture of iodine, on the other hand, is found in the medicine chest and is made by dissolving iodine crystals in alcohol. This can be used as a water purification agent if it is no more than two years old. Generally, two drops are recommended per quart of water.

According to Talal Bala'a, a PhD candidate in water hydraulics at Pasadena's Caltech, one should follow the two "Rules of Three." There is the Rule of Three for determining relative purity, and there is the Rule of Three for the process of purification.

WATER OBSERVATION RULE OF THREE
"Always begin with an obvious common sense observation of the water," states Bala'a. "Begin with three simple observations. 1. Does it look good? Is the water cloudy? Are there things in the water? 2. Does it smell good? Do you detect the odor of chemicals? Do you detect the odor of rotten material? And lastly, 3. Does it taste all right? Taste some with your tongue. Is there any astringency? Do you detect anything unpleasant?"

WATER PURIFICATION RULE OF THREE
Next, if you suspect the water is impure, follow the three fundamental steps of water purification already listed above.

"If you seriously doubt the water's purity," adds Bala'a, "you should follow the three-step process of 1. Filtering the water through a cloth, 2. Allowing the sediments in the water to settle, and then 3. Boiling the water or using chemicals. If anything is left, your body's immune system should protect you, if it can."

REALITY CHECK
You survived Hurricane Katrina or the Great Tsunami of 2004. Your neighborhood does not exist. Nothing is as you knew it the day before. You need water, and water is everywhere, but it's not safe to drink. What do you do? In such a worst-case scenario, how do you "make water?"

Years before you found yourself in such a catastrophe, it is hoped, you pondered these realities and studied books such as this.

You first must find a metal container to hold water, ideally two containers. Collect some water and let it settle. The ground water all around you has been contaminated with dead bodies (human and animal), gasoline and motor oil, and whatever else may have been in your area. As with the post-Katrina New Orleans water, it was unfit to drink and even simple distillation would not have purified it. Instead find water that has rained onto rooftops or collected in barrels and buckets.

Then how long should it settle? It all depends on what's in the water, but let it settle until some clarity appears. Then pour or siphon the water into another container, pouring it through finely woven cotton. If this is absolutely not possible, then continue to the boiling step.

This means you need to make fire. In the FIRE section, you'll learn many of the ways to make fire, some primitive, some modern. Ideally, you took the advice to *always* carry a small knife and a magnesium fire starter with you. This could be in your pocket or around your neck so you'd still have it with you after the storm subsided. Make your fire and burn whatever you can. Boil your water. Considering a worst case scenario, let it boil twenty minutes before consuming. Even this process is not 100 percent foolproof, but it will provide you a degree of safety against hepatitis A and dysentery, commonly spread in situations such as this.

Remember: Boiling generally does not deal with chemicals in the water.

Besides boiling, what other methods of water purification can be employed in an emergency? For example, what if coastal areas of the United States experienced a major tsunami, and you were one of the few survivors in a situation where fresh water was now a rarity? Or let's say you survived Hurricane Katrina and were left to your own devices for the few days to few weeks that it took for the various rescue agencies to get to you. What do you do?

PRIMITIVE WATER PURIFICATION
Beer Can Device
This method was invented and tested by Stefan Kallman in the 1980s. Despite being primitive, it turned out to be a remarkably good purifier.

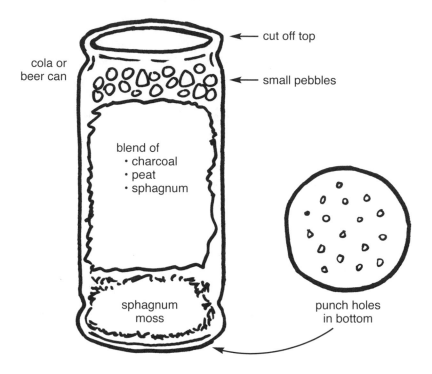

cut off top

cola or
beer can

small pebbles

blend of
• charcoal
• peat
• sphagnum

punch holes
in bottom

sphagnum
moss

You begin with an empty aluminum beer or soda can, something that is fairly common in all cities and on the fringes of most wilderness areas.

Cut off the top and punch small nail-sized holes in the bottom of the can. Put a layer of sphagnum moss in the bottom of the can. Kallman used fresh sphagnum, which is common in Europe, but you can also use sphagnum from garden supply shops.

Next, grind some charcoal until it is almost fine powder, and mix it fifty/fifty with peat, which can also be foraged or obtained at a garden supply shop. If you use barbeque charcoal for this, make certain you get the type that has no lighter fluid added to it. Add the charcoal/peat mix into the aluminum can until the can is at least two-thirds full. Finally, add a layer of small pebbles to the top. The purpose of the pebbles is simply to slow the flow of the water and to prevent channeling in the charcoal/peat medium.

In Europe where Kallman did his tests, the peat and sphagnum are common in the wild. If these materials are not common in your area, substitute something similar and experiment.

Slowly pour the suspect water into the top of the can; the pebbles slow the flow of water. The sphagnum and peat attract particulate matter, and the charcoal in the bottom absorbs any biological contaminants in the water. The first water through will appear gray, and the gray cloudiness will lessen with use.

Purify Water with Your Sock
This is another possible method where you can use a beer or soda can to purify water. I have seen it demonstrated using a tennis ball container, which is ideal because it is slightly bigger and longer than an aluminum beer or soda can. Rarely do you find a tennis ball container just lying around, however, so it is more likely you'll use a beer or soda can.

Again, cut off the top, and punch nail-sized holes in the bottom of the can. Then pack rolled-up socks (yes, clean!) into the can. Roll the socks very tightly, getting three, maybe four, socks into a can.

Pour your suspect water into the top, slowly; the water will take a while to percolate through the packed socks. The idea here is that the layers of (presumably) cotton will remove much of the particulate matter.

Remember, these are "emergency" methods when superior methods are not possible. This is by no means a 100 percent purifier.

Sand in a Can
Instead of socks in a can, take the same can as above, cut off the top and punch holes in the bottom, and fill the can with clean sand. If you do not have a source of sand that you feel is clean, there is no reason to bother with this method, as you might be making otherwise palatable water unsafe.

One way to do this sand filter is to first put a layer of cotton into the aluminum can, and then add the clean sand. The cotton will prevent sand from flowing through the holes. Slowly pour the suspect water into the top and let it flow out the bottom.

Redman, the environmental science teacher who also has a master's degree in botany, points out that these primitive methods of water

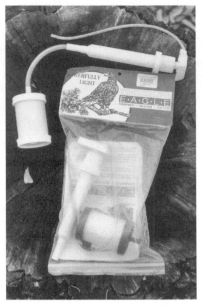

The "Press2Pure" water
purification sports bottle.

The Timberline pump filter for
water purification.

purification aren't foolproof, but provide some degree of protection if you cannot build a fire. Under normal circumstances, much of the water in wilderness areas in North America is surprisingly safe to drink, untreated. Redman points out that only on occasion does he purify the water he drinks in the high country of California's southern Sierra range. "When I'm in the high country, and there's no grazing cattle and few backpackers in the area, I have assumed that the water is safe to drink. This is especially so if the water is coming off the snow. I have never gotten sick in the Sierra. I purify the water around popular campsites. When I see a stream coming directly from melting snow, I drink it without filtering," he says.

This is in sharp contrast to health and wilderness experts worldwide who say you should always assume that open water sources are unsafe to drink, unless you find out otherwise.

When Redman is in the bush and needs to purify his water, he uses his Katadyne filter, arguably the Cadillac of water filters. Katadyne filters

Using the Timberline pump filter to obtain safe water from a small stream. DOUG HAIPT

range from backpack models (at around two hundred dollars), to much more expensive kitchen models. If you cannot afford a Katadyne, check out the water purifiers at any backpacking or sporting goods store. All these meet federal standards for their ability to remove the known harmful bacteria from water.

Solar Water Distiller
Distillation of water can be done with the sun.

The device shown in the illustration on the next page can be made small or large. It is made of plexiglass. Each cut must be made square and clean, and then glued together. The top either opens, or there is an inlet valve. As the impure water (or ocean water) evaporates, it flows down the inside of the roof and into the pure side, where there must be a valve so that water can be easily used.

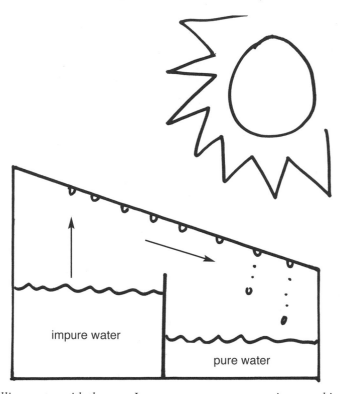

Distilling water with the sun. Impure water or seawater is poured into the left side. The sun evaporates pure water, which drips into the right side. This device can be made with glass or plexiglass. The lid must be secure, yet removable for adding new water and for cleaning. A spigot can be added to the right side.

I have also seen one made from a base of four-by-eight-foot plywood that had been waterproofed with marine resin. The lid was a sheet of rigid plastic, though a stretched sheet of plastic could also be used.

Solar Cookers International of Sacramento, California, sells a simple product for purifying water with the sun. Contact them at 1919 21st St., Suite 101, Sacramento, CA 95814, or *SolarCookers.org.*

The desert solar still is a primitive method for extracting water from the soil, but it can also be used as a way to purify suspect water—though not a very efficient way. (The details of the desert solar still are discussed on pages 21–25).

Solar Purification
Fill a clear glass container with suspect water and place it in direct sunlight for at least four hours. The UV radiation will kill the bugs in the water.

The glass must be clear—colored glass is not effective. This method only deals with living organisms in the water—not with any chemical contaminants.

We've addressed methods of purifying water, and these methods can be practiced anywhere—in the woods or in the city—assuming you have the necessary gear.

WATER SOURCES AND STORING WATER

Water is basic. Without it, there is no life. Let's take a look at the sources of water, both in town, and in the wilderness.

SOURCES

Here's the quick summary:

FINDING WATER IN THE WILDERNESS

Obvious sources
    Rain
    Springs
    Wells
    Rivers, streams, lakes, and other open sources

Not so obvious sources
    Catchments in rock
    Dew
    The ocean
    Plants
    Desert still vs. transpiration bag

FINDING WATER IN TOWN

Obvious sources
    When the tap runs dry—learn how your city gets its water
    Swimming pools
    Water heaters
    Toilet tanks
    Draining the water from a house
    Water you've stored for an earthquake

Not so obvious sources
    Collecting rainwater
    Collecting dew
    Tapping trees
    Backyard wells, where possible

Rain is a viable way to get much of your water supplies, but it has largely been ignored by most urban dwellers, city planners, and even wilderness travelers.

A friend in Pasadena, Adrian Tucker, once mounted a fifty-five-gallon drum horizontally on the backside of his garage that collected rain. Adrian then allowed the collected rainwater to drip off the garage roof down to his hillside paradise full of domestic fruit trees and wild vegetation. He quickly pointed out that fifty-five gallons is not a lot of water for his large hillside, and (before he died) he'd planned to install one or two more drums. When Adrian showed me his rain drum, he showed me the extra two-by-fours he'd installed to support the weight of the water. At 8 pounds per gallon, fifty-five gallons of water weigh 440 pounds, not including the weight of the metal drum itself.

"Make sure you do this right," said Adrian, "since it's not worth losing your roof in order to save fifty-five gallons of water."

Some of the old homes around Los Angeles built nearly a hundred years ago have rain cisterns. These were usually hillside homes, with a large underground reservoir made of fired clay or cement. Such rain cisterns were built by people who experienced hard times, and who knew that you can't always depend on outside sources for your needs. They knew that—even in the desert—rain falls sometimes and that if you plan appropriately, you can collect and use that rainwater.

With today's technologies, it would be an easy matter to build rain catchments into every home in all the western and southwestern states.

Fred Fryling, then living in Venice, California, once showed me his system for collecting his own drinking water. After it had been raining a while, he spread out a large sheet of plastic (approximately five by four feet) over some bushes in his yard. Clothes hangers secured the plastic in place. When positioned, the plastic collected rain, which ran into the spout of a nearby Sparkletts water bottle placed nearby.

Fred could fill the bottle in as little as thirty minutes during a downpour. He collected much of his coffee water and drinking water in this way.

The down spouts of this home "automatically" fill buckets with rainwater.

After the rainstorm, Fred folded up the sheet of plastic and clothes hangers and kept them in a bag: "It's just as easy to carry this in my pack while camping and collect rainwater in the woods." Fred pointed out that when camping, he would fill his cookpot and canteen with rainwater when the streams often became muddy.

Backyard Rain Catcher
The folks at WTI developed a simple "kit" for capturing rain for household use. Begin with a large, clean water bottle (plastic or glass)—at least the three-to-five-gallon size that water companies use. Set it out under a spot where the rain runs off your roof. Insert a large funnel into the top of

The WTI method of filtering and collecting rainwater.

the bottle, and cover the funnel with at least a 700 thread count cotton. The cloth will help to filter out sediment from the roof.

Do not set up such a device until after thirty-four minutes of heavy rain, after which time the bulk of the dirt and pigeon droppings will have already washed off the roof.

To obtain their easy-to-use kit, contact them at WTI, 5835 Burwood Ave, Los Angeles, CA 90042.

Desert Still vs. Transpiration Bag

Over the years we've made many desert solar stills. First dig a hole (about three feet deep by three feet wide) where there is likely to be underground

Digging a hole for a desert solar still. DUDE McLEAN

water; then place a container in the middle of the hole, surround the container with grass and cacti (if available), and cover it all with a sheet of plastic.

Though there is always some water evaporating out of the soil, location is still very important with this method. Some spots evaporate out far more water than others. Generally speaking, look for an area that appears to have been wet recently (lots of green grass, for example) or in a dry steambed (water flows in steams, and there is likely to be underground water even when the stream is dry).

Just about anything clean can be used for a container—we've even just cut off the bottom third of a plastic juice container when we had nothing else. But there are lots of suitable containers. Avoid a container with a tiny spout, as the water will not all drip down at exactly one point.

Observing the condensed mois-ture on the bottom side of the plastic covering of this desert solar still.
DUDE McLEAN

SOLAR STILL
Cross Section

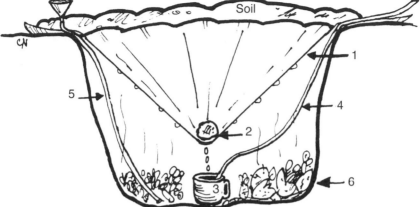

1. Sheet of plastic, five to six feet in diameter. Soil around the edges holds the plastic in place. Note the condensation on the bottom of plastic.
2. Smooth, egg-sized rock to form cone.
3. Cup to catch water.
4. Drinking tube, a quarter inch in diameter, approximately five feet long.
5. Tube to allow urine in regularly without opening still. Note funnel at top.
6. Broken cacti and other vegetation placed in hole.

Add the cactus and vegetation around the container because these plants also contain water that will evaporate out and be trapped under the plastic. Note: Use only grasses or cactus or willow, or plants that you know are nontoxic. Do not use oleander or poisonous plants as this could taint the water.

By the way, you can also pour urine into the hole, as well as ocean water (if you are near the ocean). This sort of still will evaporate out distilled water from urine or seawater. Though not an efficient way to process ocean water, it still captures some of it back in the form of distilled water.

Cover the entire hole with a sheet of plastic—Tedlar is said to be the best, but you have to do a bit of hunting to find it. If I am planning to make a solar still, I just go to a local hardware store and purchase a roll of two-mil clear plastic, typically ten feet wide. I will then cut a sheet that is ten by ten feet.

*Nathaniel Schleimer, on a WTI Desert Survival Outing, pours urine into a
desert solar still. The urine distills out as drinkable water.*

Cover the hole with the plastic and seal the edges with soil. Put a rock
in the middle of the plastic, directly over the container. This allows the
water to condense on the underside of the plastic, and drip back down into
the container. If it is a sunny day and there is sufficient moisture in the
soil, the bottom of the plastic will steam up quite quickly. If this is a bona
fide survival situation and you will be using this still to obtain your water,
you will want to put a long plastic tube (e.g., surgical tubing) into the container that is collecting water, and extending out beyond the plastic. This
allows you to suck out the water that collects, without having to remove
the plastic and lose all the heat you have built up.

Now, is all this practical? As with most things, it works best when you
really don't need it—that is, when there is plenty of moisture in the soil.
In very arid environments, with wind, we have had some stills produce
zero. Others produce just a few tablespoons. But in very moist conditions
(when we probably could have obtained all our water simply by digging a
well), we have obtained two quarts a day per still, which is quite good.

To be efficient with this, you will need a shovel, or maybe a hub cap. You'll also need the sheet of plastic and container, and probably a plastic tube.

The practicality of this method depends upon the amount of underground water where you dig, and whether or not you have a digging implement and a large sheet of clear plastic.

On the other hand . . .

Transpiration Bag

There is another simpler way to capture water, in this case not evaporating out of the soil, but evaporating out of the leaves of trees. Technically, the leaves are not "evaporating" water, but are transpiring water, part of the complex work of leaves that converts sunlight to food for the tree, and oxygen for us. *The details of this can be read in a basic biology text, or in any of a number of articles in such magazines as* American Forests.

Because this transpiration takes place continually, you might be able to capture some of that transpiring water if you have a large clear plastic bag and a short cord for tying it on.

An ideal tree is willow, but oak and eucalyptus (and many others) also have high rates of transpiration.

Find a suitable leafy branch that you can wrap in a large clear plastic bag, ideally in the sun. Wrap the branch with the bag, and tie it off with a short cord. Then wait.

We have gone into desert environments and made solar stills and installed transpiration bags so we could observe the relative results in identical weather and soil conditions, during the same allotment of time.

In all cases of this side-by-side comparison, we obtained more water with the transpiration bag than with the solar still. We are not talking about large volumes of water here. In one instance, the solar still produced about one-third cup of water in three hours, whereas the transpiration bag produced slightly more than one-half cup of water in the same time. In another case, the solar still produced about two tablespoons of water, whereas the transpiration bag produced about one-quarter cup. We've heard similar results from others as well.

So, the transpiration bag does seem to produce at least 25 percent more water than the solar still. Also, the transpiration bag is constructed with perhaps 10 percent of the labor that the solar still requires.

Transpiration bag (a clear plastic bag covering leaves to capture transpiring water).

Still, there are some reasons to consider the solar still. To a solar still, with a small funnel attached to a tube, you can continually add impure liquids (or urine, ocean water, and so forth) without opening it. This allows you to use your still, or one of your stills, as a processing device for either urine or ocean water.

Though the transpiration bag is easier to put together, there's no easy way to extract the collected water without removing the bag, pouring out the water and starting all over. Another advantage of the solar still is that—when left out overnight—it sometimes collects more water in dew *on top of the plastic* than it does under the plastic from evaporating water.

Your decision to use either method depends wholly on your location and your specific needs. Either method can be used as easily in the wilderness as in an urban backyard. Just keep in mind that you must know that the type of tree is not poisonous when using the transpiration bag. This is especially true in the city, where so many of the trees and shrubs are introduced ornamentals, some of which are toxic.

Ocean Water

We have long been taught that the largest single source of water on the earth—the oceans—is toxic and should not be drunk. Most of us have heard the horror stories about someone needing water who begins to drink ocean water, and who uncontrollably begins to drink large volumes, resulting in vomiting and diarrhea (a net water loss), and even death.

Are such stories true or false?

Take Thor Heyerdahl, for example. As a young archaeologist of the diffusionist branch of thinking, he was convinced that the oceans of the world were highways for various cultures, and not barriers to travel (as is still usually taught in colleges and universities). Among his various theories, he believed that the eastern Polynesians were populated not by those from Polynesia sailing east, but by the Indians of South America sailing west. To prove his ideas, he and his crew manufactured primitive-style reed boats and sailed the ocean's currents. He spent his life doing this, proving also that the oceans were a source of food if you knew how to capture it, as well as water, if you knew how to use it.

Despite his numerous sailing sagas—Heyerdahl's books include *Kon-Tiki, Ra Expeditions,* among others—about his travels across every major ocean in the world in primitive boats, most mainstream archaeologists still discount his ideas.

Heyerdahl wrote in *Kon Tiki* that they could extend their water supplies by mixing the stored fresh water fifty/fifty with ocean water. Neither he nor his crew experienced any ill effects from such a mix. Furthermore, he found that such water quenched the thirst much better than plain fresh water.

Rainwater and dew were also collected out in the ocean and used to fill empty water containers.

I have kept a file of stories of people lost at sea, sometimes for as long as two months. There is a very finite number of sources for food and water when you're out on the ocean, and most survivors have utilized most of these sources.

Nearly everyone who has survived being lost at sea has utilized ocean water. Typically, it had to be sipped sparingly, never large gulps. Plus, water could be drunk off the surface of a very still sea. Such water tends to be less saline. Other sources of water from the ocean, already mentioned, are rain and dew. Still another source of potable liquid—as unappetizing as it might sound—is the liquid found inside fish and water turtles. At least one more possible source of water on the ocean can be found in the inflated bladder-pods of the kelp plant. These are the round parts at the base of fronds that keep the plant afloat. If you cut one open, you'll find it nearly full of water that is not quite as saline as the ocean itself.

Now, around all major cities there are sewage treatment plants where the water is discharged into the ocean once it is "purified." In Los Angeles County, for example, sewage water flows into the Hyperion waste treatment center, a massive building full of a maze of pipes. But as large as this facility is, when it rains and there is a lot of water flowing down city streets and into the sewers to the ocean, the Hyperion waste treatment plant cannot properly process the sewage, and sewage flows into the ocean.

In such conditions, you would not want to consider drinking ocean water without some sort of processing. Nor would you even want to swim in the water under such conditions.

So is ocean water drinkable or not? The answer depends entirely on your location, and your ability to control how you consume water. Obviously, people have drunk ocean water and survived. And what of those lost at sea who did not survive? Though it is likely that some gulped ocean water and succumbed to its effects, it is also likely that death came not as a result of drinking ocean water alone. When stranded on a boat or raft in the ocean, you are subject to the intense heat and rays of the sun by day, and the intense cold and wind at night. Your clothes start to deteriorate, you get sunburned, and seasick. You may eat raw fish, and vomit. Death in the ocean is more likely a combination of exposure, hypothermia, and dehydration.

WATER STORAGE
Generally, the principles of water storage are as applicable in a wilderness cabin as in your urban garage.

Water storage containers are a bit easier to get in the city, and your source of containers may be limited in rural stores. Additionally, if you can't drive directly to your remote home, you are most likely to use those storage containers that are lightweight and can be easily carried.

Let's look at some of the materials used in water storage containers:

WATER STORAGE METHODS

	Pro	Con	Price	Comments
Glass	Glass is inert so there is nothing leaching into the container.	Glass is fragile and will break in an earthquake unless well protected.	Five-gallon water bottles can usually be purchased for a few dollars. Also, you can save any glass juice and water containers you buy, and use them for water storage.	Some of your water storage should be in glass, especially since you can get the containers for free, or next to nothing.
Metal	Durable. Some military ones are quite good.	Generally not good for long term, since they rust. Even "stainless steel" will rust in time.	This is possibly your most expensive way to go.	There are actually many choices here. Old fifty-five-gallon drums can be used, but must be cleaned well. Old water heater tanks that still hold water are also quite good.
Plastic	Inexpensive, easy to come by. Will not break in an earthquake.	Though there are "food-grade" plastics, all plastics leach something into the water. Some low-grade plastics will also crack and leak in as little as six months.	Very inexpensive. You can also save any plastic containers from juice or water and use them for your water storage.	Avoid the two-gallon plastic containers with the spigot. These are typically made of thin plastic and will spring a leak after a few months.
Clay	Inexpensive if you can make it yourself.	Must be fired to hold water. Also, subject to breakage. Be careful of lead content in clay and glazings.	Cost depends on quality of clay (crockery, ceramic, porcelain) and quality of workmanship.	Worth considering for remote areas where there is the skilled labor to make water containers.

WATER STORAGE METHODS continued

	Pro	Con	Price	Comments
Gourds	Inexpensive, can be grown in the garden, traditional.	Not for significant amounts of water for long-term storage.	Though many people in the past did use gourds for some water storage, they should be regarded as short-term storage.	Have you ever tasted water that sat in a gourd during a long hot day?? Ugh!
Other	Skins, wood, stone, and the like can all be made in remote areas.	Most of these are not viable methods for large scale, long-term water storage.		

In most parts of the world, it is wise to have an emergency water storage supply. Obviously, anyone in a desert environment where water supplies can be disrupted at any time should have water stored. Anyone in "earthquake country" should have containers of water for use in the aftermath of a major quake.

Getting Started

For earthquake preparedness, water storage is perhaps the single most important step to being prepared—and also the cheapest!

The easiest way to get started is to save all those quart and liter bottles you buy with drinks and water. Save both the plastic and the glass ones. When you're done with the juice or water, clean the container and fill it with local spring water, if available. If not available, fill it with tap water. You do not need to add drops of bleach to the tap water unless you wish to do so. The function of the bleach is to retard the growth of algae, but tap water in most parts of the country has enough chlorine already.

Store a blend of these plastic and glass containers in a box or crate—a milk-crate size box will store about twenty of these containers. Put the box in your garage or basement. Begin collecting again and just keep it up until you have a few hundred gallons of water.

The glass bottles will require no maintenance, but the plastic ones will not last forever. The best plastic containers to use for water storage are those that contained carbonated water or soft drinks. These plastics have to be strong enough to withstand the pressure of carbonization, and are made of a heavier-grade of plastic. Dude McLean, field editor of *Wilderness Way* magazine, reports that he has had plastic containers of water that lasted for at least seven years with no leakage. (He used plastic bottles that had stored carbonated water).

Another low-cost storage container is the three-to-five-gallon bakery bucket—a white plastic bucket with a lid. You can obtain these from bakeries, delicatessens, some restaurants. They can usually be obtained for free, since they are typically discarded. I have paid up to fifty cents per bucket, but usually have obtained all I needed for free.

In my parents' home, I filled about thirty of these buckets with tap water, and they were still there thirty years later. Twenty buckets were kept under the house, and out of sunlight. These buckets were fine after thirty years, and the water contained only negligible amounts of green algae. The ten buckets in the backyard patio, exposed to some sunlight, did not fare as well. A few cracked after twenty years and the water leaked out. The plastic of the rest of them was so fragile that the buckets cracked apart if not carefully handled. Most had some green algae in the water.

Conclusion: These white plastic food buckets are easy to get, cheap, and if stored in the dark, will last up to three decades.

Water Tanks

Old gas water heaters—assuming they still hold water—are excellent as a water storage device. Clean out the sediment in the bottom. You can remove the sheet metal shell and insulation, or not, but it will take up less space in your garage if the shell is removed.

Once cleaned, simply fill these up, cap them, and stand them up in the corner of your garage. Most of these hold either thirty or forty gallons of water.

Food-Grade Buckets

You can purchase food-grade plastic buckets—typically blue in color—in various sizes. The five-gallon size with the handle is very convenient, and perhaps the most economical is the thirty-gallon round bucket. Be sure to

Forty-gallon water containers (made of food-grade plastic) can be stored inconspicuously in the yard.

purchase a hand pump for the larger buckets. Buy as many of these as you can afford.

Fifty-five-Gallon Drums

Metal drums can be used for water storage, but they are best avoided if any sort of toxic chemical has been stored in the bucket. Even if these buckets were used to store oil or foods, they will still rust in time.

But fifty-five-gallon drums are so ubiquitous—and often available for the taking—that they might fit into your plans.

For example, you can position fifty-five-gallon drums under your home's downspouts and collect rainwater. The rainwater can then be used for irrigating trees and shrubs, and even for your pets and animals.

Rust ("iron") in the water will actually be good for the plants.

At a hillside home, I once took showers from a fifty-five-gallon drum. The drum was sitting on top of another drum, on a higher part of the hillside. It sat in the sun all day and got warm, so if I took the shower shortly after sundown, the water would still be somewhat hot. I just opened a spigot and took a warm shower, probably mixed with a bit of rust.

2

Fire, Lighting, Energy

FIRE

The ability to make a fire is one of the most important survival skills. On the physical side of survival skills, the mastery of fire is a must.

Granted, if everything in the city is running smoothly, you may not have the immediate need for fire making. You're still using fire, though somewhat automatically in your stove, water heater, and space heater.

But in the aftermath of an urban disaster, knowing how to safely make a fire in your backyard can be a lifesaver. The same is true for the survivors of the great Tsunami of December 2004 and Hurricane Katrina of 2005. And the same obviously applies to anyone lost in the woods.

Fire is an essential tool of survival. You should practice making a fire from scratch often and in as many possible ways as you can.

WHY FIRE?

Here's what fire does:

Cooks our food

Sterilizes water

Provides warmth (less need for shelter)

Acts as a signaling device

Useful for toolmaking (hardening wood or melting steel)

Kills bugs (as in the passive agriculture of Native Americans)

Dozens of other uses and sub-categories of the above

Here are the basic quick versions of the ways to make fire without matches. In an emergency, always start with the easiest method.

CAR BREAKS DOWN

- Use the cigarette lighter to ignite tinder.
- Use the flare in your emergency kit.
- Use the battery, with jumper cables, to create a spark.
- Use the head lamp reflector as a solar fire starter.

NO: You cannot use your mirror to make a fire.

LOST WHILE HUNTING

- Use the scope on your rifle as a magnifying glass.
- Empty a shotgun shell of shot and wadding; repack with cotton; fire.
- Empty a shotgun shell of shot and wadding; pour powder into tinder; ignite with a magnifying glass.
- Use your binoculars as a magnifying glass.

LOST IN THE WOODS

- Use your magnesium fire starter (it should ALWAYS be on your keychain).
- Use your camera lens as a magnifying glass.
- Use your flashlight batteries and steel wool.
- Use your flashlight lens reflector as a solar fire starter (maybe).
- Use the flint and steel of the pioneers.
- Try some of the most primitive Native American methods:

The hand drill	The plow
The bow and drill	The fire piston
The pump drill	

- Suggestion: Learn one new method each time you go into the woods.

BACKYARD SURVIVAL

- Use your magnesium fire starter.
- Use magnifying glasses of various sorts.
- Use a Fresnel lens (found on overhead school projectors, or can be purchased alone).
- Last resort: Use your matches or butane lighters.

There are — undoubtedly — other methods to create a fire when needed, but the above covers the gamut of the methods you would most likely employ.

The importance of fire cannot be overemphasized. The best way to continually learn new methods of fire making is to make a sport of it and work each weekend at mastering another method with friends and family. Start with the methods that require some modern tools, and gradually work your way up to the hardest methods, such as the hand drill and the plow.

Let's start with some of the backyard methods.

BACKYARD

In the aftermath of an urban disaster, it is likely you'd need to make a fire. During Hurricane Andrew, the local residents were asked to voluntarily evacuate, as the National Guard came in to protect the area. Many families refused and decided to stay with their houses. They didn't believe the storm would be that bad, and they wanted to avoid getting looted. A television crew filmed one family in an area where the power was knocked out, but their home survived. They were filmed as they sat around their backyard fire, cooking a meal and drying their clothes.

Fire is essential!

Magnesium Fire Starter

If you practice the discipline of always carrying a Doan's magnesium fire starter on your keychain, or in your purse, you will always have the means to create a fire. You should keep several in your car and in your home.

To use, you simply scrape the edge of the device until you have a pile of the silvery magnesium shavings. Then you create a spark by scraping the other end of the tool with your knife. If you carefully direct the spark into the shavings, they will ignite.

If you don't want to use your knife, you can use a small piece of a hacksaw blade or some other metallic device.

AROUND THE HOUSE

Of course, if you have dry matches, or a butane lighter, use them!

Every home should have some other sort of fire-starting device. For example, in your garage you may have a welder's sparker, used to ignite

Scraping magnesium shavings into tinder. DUDE McLEAN

a brazing torch or a welding torch. Or your kitchen may have a butane-powered clicker used to ignite the stove or fireplace.

Magnifying Device

Every home should have some sort of magnifying device. Magnifying glasses might be found in a science kit, or in the medicine cabinet (for examining splinters and wounds), or in your library for reading. Magnifying glasses are so ubiquitous that you should practice efficiently making a fire with one.

Camera

If you have a camera, you can use the lens to start a fire. A 35mm camera with a detachable lens is best, but these are becoming obsolete. Ideally, you do not want to destroy your camera in order to make a fire—though the severity of your situation might dictate that the loss of a camera is a small price to pay for fire. In some cases, you can open the back of the camera, remove the film, and allow the sun to shine through the lens.

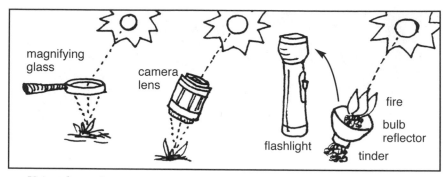

Using the sun's rays.

Flashlight

No camera? Most homes have at least one flashlight. There are two ways to make a fire with flashlights. The first uses the shiny reflector around the bulb. Disassemble the flashlight and remove this bulb. Then get some tinder—dry cotton, mugwort, a cigarette, etc. Stick the tinder into the hole in the reflector where the bulb should go, and point the reflector at the sun. On sunny days, you'll quickly have an ember or fire.

Battery and Steel Wool

The other method with a flashlight uses the batteries and steel wool. Maybe you have steel wool in your garage or workshop, or in the kitchen. Though this method can be done with one new C cell, I find it is easier with at least two D cells. Hold the two D cells as they would be in the battery, and stretch a piece of steel wool so it goes from the top of the top battery to the bottom of the bottom battery. Make the steel wool fluffy, and move it a bit. The steel wool will begin to burn. Have your tinder ready, and then ignite the tinder with the steel wool.

By the way, if you have a fresh nine-volt battery, you can simply press the battery onto steel wool and it will ignite since both poles are side by side. This is the little square battery that is sometime used to power portable radios. One way to test the relative strength of this battery is to press it on the tongue. You get an electrical shock corresponding to its strength or weakness.

Not everyone is aware that steel wool burns, and it is rather amazing to see it for the first time. One of my students once told our class a story about

Making fire with a D battery and steel wool.

steel wool. He had a loud muffler on his motorcycle, but he needed to make a short trip one night. He had planned to repair the muffler in a few days, and just wanted to muffle the loud noise so he would not get stopped by a police officer. His brilliant idea was to pack the muffler with steel wool that he had in his garage. As he drove off into the night, the muffler was clearly quiet. As he turned back to look at the police sirens approaching him, however, he saw a long stream of sparks shooting out his muffler into the dark of the night. He discovered that night how steel wool burns!

CAR BREAKS DOWN
You're traveling on a back road and your car breaks down. Or you run out of gas. You're going to spend some time there until you can repair the car or attract attention to yourself.

Unless it is a very short distance to the main highway or a town, it is best to stay with your car. The car is more visible, and at least you have some supplies there.

How can you make fire with items that are either a part of, or in, your car?

Begin with the cigarette lighter. Get some tinder ready, press in the lighter, and then press the tinder into the lighter. It shouldn't take too long to get a fire this way.

Some new cars do not have "cigarette lighters." When I inquired why, I was told "not everyone smokes." Every car should have a cigarette lighter—it is a good emergency device for fire starting. And whether or not you smoke, the twelve-volt outlet is needed for an array of devices such as spotlights, air pumps, vacuums, and so forth.

You should have flares in your emergency kit. Flares are easy to ignite by striking, and they burn for at least 15 minutes, guaranteeing a campfire in all but the very worst conditions.

No cigarette lighter? No flares? Try the battery. Keep in mind that batteries are exploded and damaged all the time by people who don't take the time to read how to properly give a jump charge from one car to another. You'll be using your jumper cables to get a fire with your battery, and you'll want to take all precautions to avoid an accident.

Ideally, remove the battery from the car. Attach the two ends of the jumper cables to the battery as you would if you were going to give a jump. Next, prepare a pile of tinder. This could be cotton, rags, finely crushed leaves, cattails, and the like. Do not just quickly hit the two free

Using a car battery and jumper cables to ignite tinder.

Using a Jeep's headlamp reflector to focus the sun's rays and make fire.
DUDE McLEAN

ends of the jumper cables together, as this could result in battery damage. Rather, slowly bring the two ends together into the tinder. You should get an electrical arc from each end of the copper cable. If your tinder is good, it will ignite.

If you cannot do any of the above, there is also the reflector around the headlamp. This will be a bit harder to remove than the reflector of a flash-light, but a car's reflector is much larger. You'll probably need a screw-driver to remove the covering that holds the reflector in place. You'll be glad you invested in that Swiss Army knife. Once the headlamp is free, you'll need to break the glass. (Obviously, you don't want to do this if you have any hope of driving out on your own).

NOTE: Not all cars have a reflector that is useful in this way. I have used the Jeep headlamp successfully, since it is relatively large and round. A reflector that is not round (from a modern car) will not work, so don't ruin the headlamp.

Aim the reflector at the sun, while inserting a bit of tinder into the focal point of light. You have to move the reflector and tinder around a bit to find the focal point, and I'd recommend wearing sunglasses while doing this. On a sunny day, you'll get a flame quickly.

By the way, the headlamp reflector on most Jeeps is nearly ideal for this, as it is relatively large, round, and easy to remove. Some cars have headlamps that are hard to remove. Others have rectangular reflectors, which will not work, so don't bother ruining them.

Can you use your mirror for making a fire? You might want to try it for yourself. Though it makes a great signalling device, there is no way you can make a fire with it, unless you do something like breaking the glass into little pieces and then gluing them back together on the surface of a parabolic dish. In an emergency, there are better ways to make a fire.

LOST WHILE HUNTING

If you're out hunting, you *should* also carry basic camping gear, which includes several ways to make a fire. You should automatically be carrying a Doan's magnesium fire starter. But let's say you left home in a hurry, or you somehow lost your fire gear. Now what? You still have your rifle or shotgun.

Do you still have your binoculars? If so, you can use them as a magnifying glass to make fire during the day. If you have never tried this, then practice. Don't wait till an emergency is upon you.

If you have a rifle, do you have a scope? If so, you can also use that scope as a magnifying glass.

Were you out shooting bird with the shotgun? Take one shotgun shell and open the top. With today's plastic shell cases, you will probably need your knife to open the top of the shell. Remove the shot and wadding. Pour the powder onto some tinder. If you have a magnifying glass, you can now ignite that tinder.

No magnifying glass? Take that shell with the shot and wadding removed, and pack some cotton into the shell. Close it back up and fire it into a pile of tinder in a safe place. The cotton should come out as a glowing ember. Add your prepared tinder, and you should have a fire in no time.

LOST IN THE WOODS

Any of the other methods already described *might* be viable methods for getting a fire, depending on what you happen to be carrying in your pack. You *should* at the very least have a magnesium fire starter with you.

If you didn't have any of the modern devices with you that would allow you to make a fire, perhaps you can get a fire with the traditional flint and steel.

Flint and Steel

You will need a steel. This can be a steel made by a blacksmith for the express purpose of fire making. Or it can be the piece of an old file. Or it can be the back of a carbon steel knife. But a piece of an old file is probably the easiest to obtain.

Next you need flint, or some "sparkable" stone. You don't need to be a geologist to identify flint or usable stone. There is no flint in my immediate vicinity, but there is plenty of quartzite and other sparkable stones. To test whether or not certain stones are sparkable, hold a piece in your left hand, and sharply strike it with the file in your right hand. If there is a good shower of sparks, the rock can be used.

You have the stone, you have the steel, and now you need some ideal tinder. In this case, you could spark into some fluffed-up dry cattail heads. The cattail is so fluffy that it flies all over as you attempt to do this. But it *can* be done, and when the cattail ignites, watch out so you don't lose your eyelashes.

Tinders must be ideal in order to get a spark to stick, and to get a fire. Traditionally, char cloth was used. To make char cloth, you first need a small metal tin, such as a tea can or a breath mint tin. Cut pieces of cotton to fit into the tin, and close the lid. Punch a small nail-size hole in the lid of the tin. Put the tin into the fire, and let it smoke for ten minutes or more. When you retrieve the can, the cotton will be all black and ideal for use with the flint and steel.

Oh, you noticed that you had to put the tin into the fire—something you can't do if you don't have a way to make a fire in the first place. Yes, this is a method that necessitates one of the basic survival tenets: *planning ahead.* If you haven't planned ahead and made char cloth, you'll need to try to get your flint and steel fire with cattails, shredded bark, or other natural tinder.

To get a fire with the flint and steel, there are many ways to hold each, and many ways to do the striking. Here is the way I do it—the way I was taught by Barton Boehm one Thanksgiving Day afternoon. I hold the quartzite in my left hand between my thumb and first finger. I have a piece of char cloth between my first and second finger. Holding the steel in my

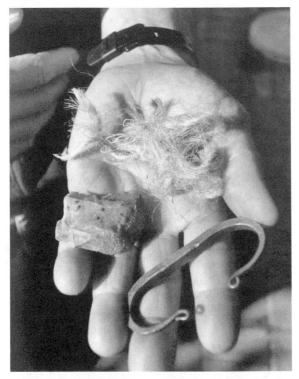

Clockwise from bottom: steel, flint, and tinder. DOLORES LYNN NYERGES

Here's one way to hold the flint and tinder for striking. DOLORES LYNN NYERGES

right hand, I sharply strike the quartzite. The strike is not a hit; rather, it is a sharp strike with the steel moving perpendicular to the stone. I strike on an edge of the quartzite. If done correctly, a shower of sparks flies, and hopefully, a few will fall onto the char cloth and cause a section of it to glow. You then take that glowing char cloth, surround it with tinder, and blow it into a flame.

Ah, but you have no steel. You will need to use one of the friction methods utilized by aboriginal peoples for thousands of years. The fire piston requires too much setup to be of use in a survival situation, and so does the pump drill, so we won't address those.

With the fire plow, Tom Hanks successfully made his fire in *Castaway*. The plow is done by simply rubbing one stick back and forth onto a flat log or piece of wood. Though there are many people out there who can do this—and it is popular in the Polynesians—I still find that it requires more strength than I can muster. In real life, it would be quite doubtful that Tom Hanks would fail at the hand drill, and then succeed at the more difficult fire plow.

For most of us, the hand drill or the bow and drill are the primitive methods of choice.

Hand Drill

The hand drill requires only two pieces of wood—the drill and the hearth. Ideal woods are cottonwood, willow, mulefat, cedar, and many others.

The drill is about eighteen inches long and about as thick as a pencil. The hearth should be flat on the bottom so it doesn't wobble when you drill. You cut a little triangular notch on the side, and begin drilling at the tip of the notch.

To drill, you put your left foot on the hearth (assuming right-handedness), and position the drill in a small hole you gouged into the hearth at the tip of the triangular notch. You'll be kneeling on your right foot, and spinning the drill with both hands. You begin at the top, and focus on downward pressure more than speed. As your hands go downward, you bring them back up and begin from the top again. Or you have a few friends working with you, and when your hands go to the bottom, someone else takes over drilling from the top.

You continue until you get smoke, and then dust starts to accumulate in the triangular notch. Depending on your skill level, and persistence, you

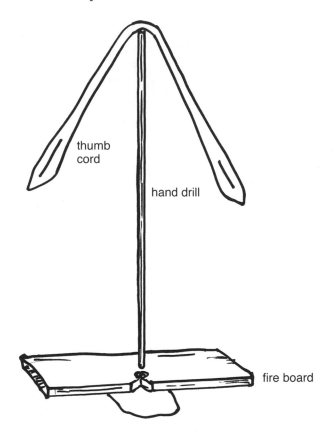

should get an ember to develop in the dust in anywhere from a few minutes to several hours.

When you get an ember, you carefully place it into some prepared tinder (a nest of mugwort, shredded bark, and so forth) and blow on it so it grows. You envelop the tinder bundle with pine needles or dry grass, and continue to blow until you get a flame. Watch your eyebrows!

My first attempts to do this by myself were unsuccessful. My arms were exhausted, and I was frustrated.

Thumb Cord

The very first time I got a coal by myself was because I was using a thumb cord. The thumb cord has many variations. I use a strip of horsehide about two feet long, with a slit on each end for my thumbs. You put your thumbs

The long straight stalks of mule fat are ideal for hand drills. DUDE McLEAN

A student in a survival skills class works on making a fire with the hand drill. DUDE McLEAN

into the slits, and place the middle of the horsehide strip over the top of the drill. By using this thumb cord, you are applying pressure to the top of the drill, which is good, and your hands will stay in one place, which is also good, sort of. Since the thumb cord provides an advantage over the bare hands alone, I have used it numerous times with success. But it does force your hands into an uncomfortable position, which I don't like, but can tolerate. You would only use the thumb cord if you were by yourself, since this method does not allow another person to join in and help.

So, whenever I am with a group, I prefer no thumb cord so everyone can join in.

By the way, this was probably the single most widely used primitive fire-starting method throughout history. It was the method of choice throughout most of North America when only the Indians ruled the land. And though it may seem terribly difficult to someone who has not done it, keep it mind that children in the old days would have mastered this by age ten or so.

As for the record time in producing a coal by the hand drill, Alan Halcon of Southern California has produced a coal in 6.5 seconds. He has written a booklet describing how he does it, and how correct body posture makes a difference. See his booklet at *TheHandDrill.com.*

Bow and Drill
The bow and drill takes a little longer to set up, but is a bit easier for most folks to get a fire. There is the hearth as before, and also the drill. The drill in this case is shorter—rarely more than a foot, and as thick as your thumb. There is also a hand block for holding the drill in place at the top. This can be a rock with a hole in it, a piece of soapstone, a bone, a galvanized pipe cap, or a piece of hardwood into which you've gouged a little hole. You should soap or oil the hole for the hand block, since you do not want friction here.

And there is also the bow, with which the drill is spun. The bow can be any wood, straight or curved, and it could also be a bone (I have seen people use ribs), and perhaps even other materials. I generally use a piece of willow or alder for the fire bow, about as thick as my thumb. For length, I put the stick in my armpit, and measure out to my wrist, and cut to that length. Then you need a cord for the bow, which can be parachute cord, shoe strings, woven yucca fiber, and the like.

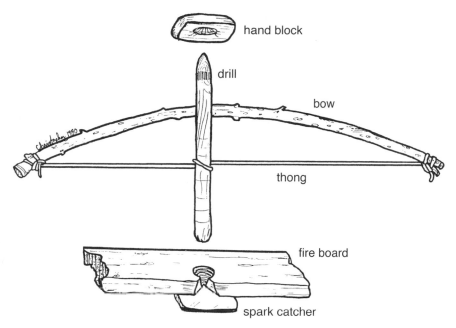

Fire by friction.

When everything is ready, you twist the bow string around the drill. It should be snug—not so loose that it slips, but not so tight that you can barely turn the drill.

You kneel on your right knee, with your left foot holding down the hearth (assuming right-handedness). You put the drill into the hole in the hearth, hold the top of the drill with the hand block in your left hand, and carefully begin to drill with your right hand. If everything goes well, you may have a coal in a few minutes. But everything rarely goes right . . .

The drill flips out and you have to start over. The cord breaks, so you get a new cord. Maybe you drill all the way through the hearth before getting a coal, so you make a new hole. Lots of things can go wrong, but you persist, and soon you have a coal, which you put into your prepared tinder, and now, you have done it. Fire! You are part of the Secret Society of Fire Makers. Donning your loincloth and running around the campground, you scream like Tom Hanks that you have made fire. That's the ritual.

I had tried to make fire by this method, using Larry Dean Olsen's *Outdoor Survival Skills* book as my guide, hundreds of time before I finally

The author demonstrates the use of the bow and drill for fire starting.
DUDE McLEAN

succeeded. One Sunday afternoon, I decided I would not quit until I succeeded. It took me three and a half hours to get that coal, and I did it with the most unlikely components: my drill was an old broomstick, and the hearth was a piece of African mineral wood that I was saving for a knife handle. These were unsuitable fire materials, and yet I made the coal in spite of my ignorance. Once I learned about willow and cottonwood, all my fire-making efforts almost seemed easy.

Other Primitive Methods
Friends, there really are *many* ways to create a fire. Although we are addressing the most viable methods in this book, here are a few comments on some of the other methods you may have heard about. The fire saw is regarded as quite difficult by most who have tried it. You cut a dry piece of bamboo into a saw shape, and then you saw onto another piece of dry bamboo that is perpendicular to the saw. You saw and you saw and you saw, and it is best done with two people.

I regard the plow as extremely difficult, though children have done it with ease when they have the right woods and have the right touch. Essentially, you are rubbing one dry piece of wood (could be as thick as your thumb and thicker, and maybe two feet long) onto a larger dry piece of

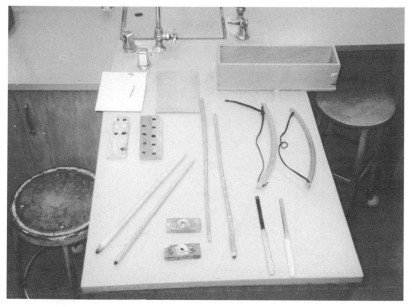

Hearths, drills, bows, and handholds from Jonathan Stamper's students.
JONATHON STAMPER

Note how the dust accumulates in the notch. In that dust you'll get your coal. DUDE McLEAN

PUMP DRILLS

FOR FIRE

FOR DRILLING
HOLES

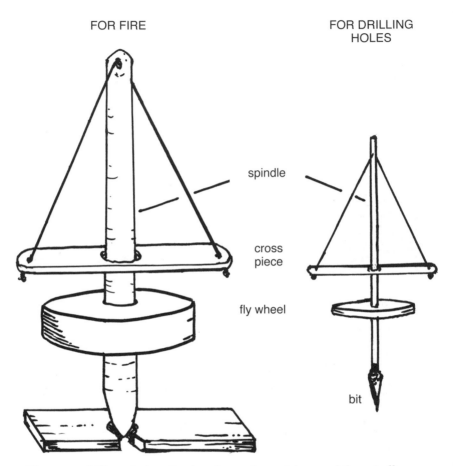

spindle

cross
piece

fly wheel

bit

The pump drill works by allowing the cord to twirl around the spindle, and then pushing down on the cross piece. The flywheel keeps the spindle moving, and the cords twirls back around the spindle. The user simply pushes down.

The more common pump drill is for drilling holes in shells, wood, and the like. The bit can be a knapped stone, a nail, or other similar object.

The pump drill for making fire must have a heavier flywheel, typically made of stone. In general, the pump drills for making fire are much larger than those used for drilling holes.

wood or log. Your angle must be just so, and you must watch the dust pile that accumulates and begins to produce prolific smoke. Eventually, some sort of magical alchemical process occurs and all of a sudden you have a coal, which you then transfer into your tinder and blow into a flame. If you want to succeed at the plow, buy Robin Blankenship's book, *Earth Knack,* and study her chapter on fire.

The fire piston is practiced in certain South Pacific islands, as well as by many of today's primitive skills practitioners. You have a rod that fits exactly into a tube. You put some tinder in the tube, insert the rod and whack it, and the compressed oxygen gets hot and ignites the tinder, if all goes well. The fire piston, however, must be made to a high degree of precision for it to work, so you are unlikely to consider making one in a survival situation. And even under ideal conditions, this takes a bit of work to consistently get a coal. If you're interested in learning this method, buy one from one of the many sources available on the internet and practice.

The pump drill is another viable way to make a fire. The pump drill is more often used to drill holes in shell, wood, and the like. But the pump drill can also be used to make a fire. Generally, it needs to be larger, and the flywheel must be heavier (or weighted with stones) in order for it to work. You use it on the same sort of hearth that you'd use for the bow and drill. You begin pumping, only pressing down. The weight of the flywheel keeps it spinning back up, and you just keep pressing down after each up-movement. But if you're doing this to make fire, the resistance increases, and without a heavy (or very large) flywheel, there will not be the speed generated to make fire.

The pump drill is a fascinating tool to make for science camp or for children in the woods to drill holes in shells to make jewelry. But it really isn't the top choice of a fire-making device unless you're willing to make it bigger and heavier. This means that there is a lot more setup involved. Your time is best spent on one of the other methods, especially in a survival situation.

Here is an overview of the many ways you can make a fire without matches. We've started with the most difficult primitive methods, and then addressed various modern methods. If any details are unclear, read the text, or consult the listed references. P.S. *YES,* there are many other ways to start a fire besides what is listed here. These are the basics.

ALTERNATIVE WAYS TO MAKE FIRE

Method	Pro	Con	Comments
Fire plow	Rub a drill back and forth onto a baseplate.	Simple to set up—requiring two unfinished pieces of wood.	For most people, requires great strength.	Practiced in Hawaiian and Polynesian islands.
Hand drill	Spin a long pencil-shaped piece of wood onto a baseplate.	Very simple to set up.	Requires good stamina and muscle strength, or several people.	Once the main method of fire-making by most Native Americans.
Hand drill with thumb cord	A cord connected to each thumb pressed down on the drill.	Provides consistent pressure on the drill, so the hands don't have to stop drilling.	Forces the hands outward somewhat.	The ideal way to practice and master the hand drill.
Bow and drill	A drill is spun with a bow and cord, pressed (via a handpiece) onto a baseplate.	This technology makes it relatively simply for most people to make a fire.	Requires more time to set up.	You can buy Boy Scout kits to do this.
Pump drill	The drill has an attached flywheel, and a cross bar attached to a cord. The cross bar is pumped up and down.	When you have the right woods, and a heavy flywheel, this is a remarkably easy way to get a fire.	This requires significantly more time to get all the parts just right.	Pump drills— with a bit—are used to make holes in things like jewelry and bull-roarers.
Fire piston	A rod, fitted into a cylinder, is whacked hard. The air compresses, igniting tinder.	Assuming all is just so, this can be a reliable and quick way to get a fire.	However, if the rod isn't perfectly fitted to the cylinder, you will be very frustrated with this method.	Due to the necessary precision in construction, this is not usually a tool you'd make in the wild.

ALTERNATIVE WAYS TO MAKE FIRE continued

	Method	Pro	Con	Comments
Flint and steel	With a steel, strike flint or quartz to create sparks, which are directed into tinder.	Relatively simple to do.	Must have ideal tinder, such as char cloth.	Once common in Europe, Asia, and parts of Africa.
Magnesium fire starter	A modern device. Scrape magnesium shavings into tinder, and spark with a built-in striker.	Enables you to always have a reliable fire starter on your keychain.	Must also have a knife. (You *do* carry a knife, don't you?)	The best, cheapest, and easiest modern fire-starting method.
Blast force	A fancy device that produces a big spark.	This really impresses your friends.	Overpriced.	Save your money!
Magnifying glass (e.g., Fresnel lens, camera lens, rifle scope)	Focus the sun's rays to a point in tinder.	Wholly practical during daylight hours.	Needs ideal tinder.	Can even be done with clear ice.
Reflectors (flashlight or headlamp)	Put tinder where the bulb would be and point at sun.	Excellent backup fire-starting method.	May permanently ruin a flashlight or headlamp.	Gets a quick flame on a sunny day.
Flashlight batteries	Stretch fine steel wool from pole to pole.	Incredibly easy way to get a fire.	Batteries must be fresh; may quickly deplete battery's charge.	Only useful if you happen to have steel wool.
Car battery	Remove battery from car, attach jumper cables, slowly bring free ends together into tinder.	With ideal tinder, somewhat easy way to get a fire in emergencies.	Must be careful when bringing cables together so battery doesn't explode.	Before you do this, use your flares or cigarette lighter.

LIGHTING

It is rare that I even bother to carry a flashlight into the wilderness. This is not because I do not value the remarkable invention of the handheld flashlight. I think the flashlight is a great tool, and indispensable around the home where you can properly maintain it.

Perhaps it is just me, but I have found that flashlights in the pack, and on the trail, have a high rate of failure. Maybe sand gets into the threads, or the batteries go dead, or it drops and the bulb fails.

For awhile, I carried those little hand-held pump flashlights. They have no batteries, and the bulbs rarely burn out. But I found them too inconvenient. They were good only for any job that required one hand, since you have to constantly pump them for light. Plus, they were too much like toys, and did not hold up to the rigors of the trail.

There are other reasons why I never got hooked on flashlights. Since I generally plan my wilderness trips in advance, I attempt to work during the available daylight, whether summer or winter. Sometimes, I will plan trips to coincide with the full moon so we have a convenient "night light."

I also learned that human eyes can adjust remarkably well to the dark. Depending on the individual, it may take thirty minutes to an hour for the eyes to get acclimated to the dark so that you can function somewhat normally. (As one ages, this night vision may be steadily diminished). Everything will seem approximately black and white, but you will be able to see.

Our eyes are built differently than an owl's, so we can never achieve their complete ability to see in the dark. Still, we can achieve functional visibility in the dark if we allow our eyes to adjust.

If you must have lighting, let's look to the past for solutions.

There is, of course, the ubiquitous campfire, which can provide lighting in a somewhat limited manner.

The manufacture of lamps goes way back in time. One example is the Middle Eastern oil lamp, many examples of which are still extant today.

The simplest oil lamp is also called the slush lamp. Any bowl that will hold oil can be made into a slush lamp. I have made them from a piece of soapstone into which a hollow was carved. I have made them from coconut halves. I have seen examples in clay, stone, metal, glass, and even bone. Anything that holds oil can be made into a lamp.

A coconut shell slush lamp with a rolled piece of dried mullein as a wick

A view of the first-year rosette of mullein.

You need to create a wick from suitable material, and then find a way to stand it vertically in the oil. I have used a bit of cotton for a wick, as well as a rolled piece of a mullein leaf. To hold the wick upright, I have weighted it on the bottom with a paper clip, a rock, a little nut or bolt, and the half of a wild black walnut shell.

I typically will half-fill a coconut shell with oil, add the wick, and light the wick. The slush lamp must be able to sit flat, and be out of the wind.

Though I have used cheap vegetable oil from the store, in the wild your main source of oil will be from the fat of an animal.

If you have no animal oil, you should probably try another method. Depending on your location and your knowledge of plant identification, however, and the abundance of certain plants, it is possible to extract sufficient oil from plants. For example, you can gather a large volume of black walnuts, crush them, and boil them (which requires a large pot). Or, you can boil large volumes of bayberry (leaves or nuts), common in the Pacific Northwest. In some cases, you can get sufficient oil by boiling mature wild sunflower heads. In all cases, the oil comes to the surface of the water and you skim it off.

Or you can try a primitive torch for your lighting needs. There are many variations of the torch. A dried cattail spike can serve as a torch, though it functions better if first dipped in oil, pine pitch, or similar material.

Small rolls of birch bark have also been used in the past as a torch. Birch bark is very flammable. It is rolled or folded into what will appear as very large cigars. It must be wrapped or sewn so it will stay together.

Whether or not such a torch is viable is entirely dependent upon what sort of natural materials you can find in your area.

URBAN APPLICATION

At home, flashlights are far more viable as a dependable source of emergency or off-the-grid lighting. You should mount them on the wall near your door so they are always handy when you need them. Buy the best you can afford. You cannot go wrong with MagLites, for example, and other flashlights used by the police, such as SureFire.

For maximum self-sufficiency, get a flashlight whose batteries (or battery pack) can be easily recharged. Also, invest in a solar-powered battery charger. A good one will cost under a hundred dollars, and will be capable of recharging C- and D-cell batteries in a few hours on a sunny day. For nearly ten years, I used the same nickel-cadmium batteries in my 4 D-cell flashlight and kept recharging the batteries when weak.

Solar chargers give you more options in a survival setting, and they are more widely available from backpacking stores and retail outlets like Real Goods now that solar electricity is starting to get mainstream.

The LED flashlights are also worth considering, especially since the LED lights last longer than the more common incandescent bulbs. The little Photon Micro-Light II uses LED and fits on the keychain. These definitely have their place.

If you're in the market for some new flashlights and lighting devices, seriously consider the headlamp. These are not just for cave explorers, as they allow you to use your hands and have lights at night. In the aftermath of an earthquake, a headlamp can be a valuable tool in the dark.

Another traditional form of lighting is candles. All the pioneers to the United States made their own candles. Candle making is an easy skill worth practicing. You melt the wax, dip your wick into the wax, let it dry, dip again, and continue until you have a candle. You can also use molds, such as old frozen juice containers.

Still, if you live in an urban area, candles are easy to come by and are inexpensive—as long as you don't try to buy them after a big earthquake has severed your electric lines.

After a blackout that affected much of Southern California in the late 1980s, my friend Nathaniel immediately rushed down to the local supermarket. They were sold out of candles. He then went to a local department store. This time, all the cheap utility candles were sold out, and they were selling the fancy candles for three times their normal selling price. Nathaniel told me this story as my kitchen and living room were well-lit from candles and Aladdin oil lamps—all purchased long before the blackout.

As for oil lamps, they are good to have, and there are many to choose from. If you have a tight budget, purchase them at yard sales and thrift stores. In the cities, they are undervalued and you will nearly always pay less than their actual value if you shop around.

Since they can break in an earthquake, you will need to pack them well when not in use. Also, you must store extra lamp oil, as well as a few wicks.

If you have the budget to afford it, you can purchase some panels that bring light into your home via the magic of fiber optics. You will have no light during the night from this source, as the fiber optic cables are simply routing sunlight into your home. Still, they render you slightly more free of the grid.

Let's not forget the Amish people from Ohio, Pennsylvania, and surrounding areas. Since they shun electricity entirely, their lighting during the night comes from oil lamps. They build their homes and workshops with large south-facing windows so they do not need to have lighting during the day.

ENERGY

COOKING

It is a wonderful experience to enter the wilderness with no cooking gear and to cook your food as peoples of the past did, without stainless steel or aluminum cookware. Many foods can be cooked or warmed on flat rocks propped up on other rocks over a fire. Many Native Americans of the past cooked on flat pieces of soapstone or sandstone in this way, sometimes oiling the stone as city folk might oil their cast iron skillet.

Some foods can be cooked around the perimeter of the campfire or directly in the ashes. Depending on what is being cooked, it may need to be wrapped in leaves first.

I've cooked corn, potatoes, yam, biscuits, yucca fruit, even meat in this manner. Sticks can be propped up around the campfire, or the coals, and the food items cooked thereon.

If a vessel for holding liquid is required, such as in soup or tea, you can usually find a discarded soda can just about anywhere in today's world. Cut off the top and you have your cooking vessel, though small.

If the trash of modern man has not found its way into your neck of the wilderness, you can once again look to the past for a cooking solution.

Native Americans of the West Coast carved cooking pots from the relatively soft soapstone. At the Southwest Museum in northeast Los Angeles, I have seen large soapstone pots capable of holding several gallons. But such works of art take a long time to carve, and in an immediate survival situation, you might be able to carve, or peck, a suitable hollow into a rock in a matter of hours. Propped up into the fire, this may serve as your backwoods cooking pot.

In the premetal days, peoples of the past also used cooking stones. These were typically very smooth cobblelike stones, about an inch or two in diameter. These were put into the fire to heat, and then were carefully removed from the fire with tongs. They would be dropped into wooden bowls to heat water or soup. Depending on how much water you were trying to heat, and how hot you managed to get the stones, you could effectively heat soup or stew this way.

I have used small squares of soapstone as cooking rocks. Each piece of soapstone had a hole drilled through it so that I could extract it from the fire by inserting a green stick into it, and then carefully plop it into the liquid in the wooden bowl.

In Australia, the Aborigines have long made a type of pancake from ground mulga (a type of acacia) seeds. Once they had mixed the flour with water and created a dough of just the right consistency, they would lay the large pancake—called damper—directly onto the ash of a cooling campfire. Many still make damper today by this same method, though they tend to use white flour.

Cooking some acorn squares on a flat slate suspended on bricks.

Venison cooks on a piece of flat soapstone. Stinging nettles cook in the can.
DUDE McLEAN

Cooking without modern supplies is not difficult. It is what people did for thousands of years. Yet it is amazing to me every time I encounter a group of Boy Scouts camping out somewhere, cooking entirely with the stoves they carried in from home. It is as if they have forgotten the simple art of cooking over an open fire.

In the urban environment, a woodstove makes sense because it can be used for cooking if the gas or electricity is out. But if your budget does not allow the purchase of a safe indoor woodstove, you can still improvise simple cooking methods in your backyard in the event of some urban disaster.

If you have a barbecue—either a built-in cement one or a metal one— then you have a way to cook. Typically, the biggest obstacle facing the backyard cooker is lack of fuel. If you're hooked on charcoal briquettes, perhaps you should learn to use little twigs, tree prunings, scraps of paper, scrap wood, and other material that you are likely to have in abundance in any urban location.

Gary Gonzles (left) and the author enjoy a winter fire in the forest. DUDE
McLEAN

*An old woodstove
makes a decorative
outdoor cooker.*

A fifty-five-gallon drum that has been converted into the "central heating" in this Navajo hogan.

No barby?

One of the simplest backyard stoves is a circle of flat stones or bricks, on a safe surface, covered with a grill of some sort. Build a fire and cook.

Backpacking stores are full of a broad variety of large and small backpacking stoves, all of which could be pressed into service if your conventional stove were unavailable.

I like one called the Pyramid, invented by a Pasadena, California, man. It folds flat so it stores and packs easily. It opens up into what looks like an inverted pyramid into another pyramid. You add charcoal or wood to it and cook on the top. I have cooked many backyard meals on this slim little stove.

Ernest Hogeboom, now living in Turlock, California, has built numerous stoves from large discarded cans. Some had smoke holes, and some did not. Typically, the fire would be built inside the can. You'd simply put your pot or pan on top of this stove and cook away, hobo dining at its best.

But if you dare not reveal your whereabouts with the smoke, a solar cooker is the way to go. If you have one in your garage, such as the model made by Solar Cookers International, then use it!

I made one of these solar cookers back in the mid-1970s, using plans found in the *Mother Earth News* magazine. The cooker still works!

Otherwise, you can make a simple solar cooker with two boxes, a sheet of glass, some duct tape, and some old newspapers.

Jerry O'Dell (left) and Dolores Lynn Nyerges examine the Pyromid cooker.

Actor Ed Begley, Jr. and child wait for hot tea from the Solar Cooker (by Solar Cooker International).

A solar oven made in the mid-1970s from plans in the magazine Mother Earth News.

How to Make a Cardboard Box Solar Oven

There is an inexpensive solar cooker that can be constructed in an hour with discards. In certain parts of the world, the solar oven is viable year-round. Throughout the West, Southwest, and Southern U.S. states, such an oven is useful throughout most of the year. In the Northern and Northeastern states, such a solar cooker is still practical at least six months out of the year, and maybe more. It can easily be carried in the car for camping trips.

Here's how you make it.

First, get two cardboard boxes, one being about two inches larger than the other in all dimensions. You can get these for free behind markets, or

Supplies required for a simple solar oven: A smaller box that fits into a larger box, some newspaper, aluminum foil, duct tape, a few empty tuna cans, and a pane of glass.
TIMOTHY SNIDER

Taping the tuna cans into the bottom of the larger box. This prevents the smaller box from compressing the newspaper underneath and thus losing insulation. TIMOTHY SNIDER

Packing newsprint for insulation around the tuna cans. TIMOTHY SNIDER

you can buy them at stationery stores. You could also just start with sheets of cardboard, and cut and tape the pieces until you have the two boxes.

Begin by sealing the edges of the two boxes with masking tape or duct tape. Then insert four small empty cat food or tuna cans in the bottom of the larger box. Place the smaller box into the large box to see how it fits. Line the inside of the smaller box with aluminum foil, folding it in carefully so it stays secure. With the smaller box inside the larger one, the top edges of both boxes should be at the same level.

Next, pack the space between the two boxes with crumpled newspapers. First pack the bottom. As you may have guessed, the purpose of the cat food cans is to keep the inner box from collapsing all the way down to the outer box, thus losing the value of the insulation.

When the space between the boxes is completely filled with crumpled newspapers, tape everything down so it's all very neat. Then cut pieces of cardboard and tape it over the open space between the tops of the two boxes. Now we need a lid.

The lid can be made in a variety of ways. All you need is a wood or cardboard frame that fits securely and snugly over the top. This lid must

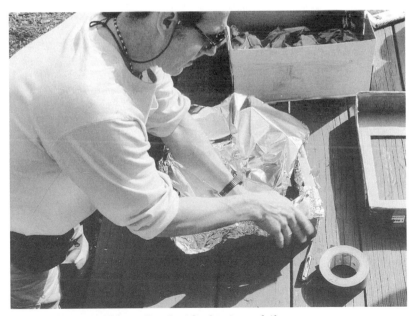

The smaller inner box is lined with aluminum foil. TIMOTHY SNIDER

The smaller box is now carefully placed into the larger box. TIMOTHY SNIDER

The space on top between the two boxes is covered with duct tape.
TIMOTHY SNIDER

An opening, which is the size of the inner box, is cut in the lid.
TIMOTHY SNIDER

go over the outer, or larger, box. To make things easier, I generally try to find the larger box that already has a lid, as opposed to a box where the four flaps fold down for the top. But if your box doesn't already have a lid, one is easily made with tape and scissors.

Then you cut a hole in the lid corresponding to the size of the inner cardboard box. This hole is covered with a sheet of plastic or glass. Glass is obviously better, so in order to keep the cost down, get a piece of glass from a discarded door or window. They are easy to come by on trash day in any city.

That's it! There are a few improvements and refinements, but this simple box solar cooker as described here can be made by anyone, and it works quite well.

Almost ready to put on the lid. TIMOTHY SNIDER

Putting on the lid to see how it fits. TIMOTHY SNIDER

Since this is just a rectangular box, we usually prop one end of it up so the glass faces the sun more directly. Also, though you don't really need a reflector for this solar oven, we have made simple reflectors that also serve as a protection for the glass. Just take a piece of cardboard slightly larger than the glass on the lid. Cover it with aluminum foil, with the shiny side out. This is your reflector. Then secure one end of this reflector to the lid, so that you can lift the reflector up as needed to shine more sunlight into the box. We also typically add a string to the free end of the reflector so we can pull the reflector to the position we want it, and then secure the string with another little piece of tape.

The thing to keep in mind with a solar cooker is that you should prepare lunch at breakfast time, and dinner at lunch time. Solar cookers take a few hours to cook a meal, and burning is impossible.

Solar cooking has many advantages. For one thing, your kitchen will stay cooler in the summer. There is very little fuss. You just put things in the oven, occasionally turn the oven to be sure it's facing the sun, and then have your meal a few hours later. Plus, there is no fire—something

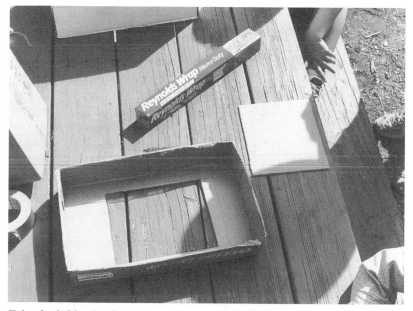

Take the lid back off to tape on the pane of glass. TIMOTHY SNIDER

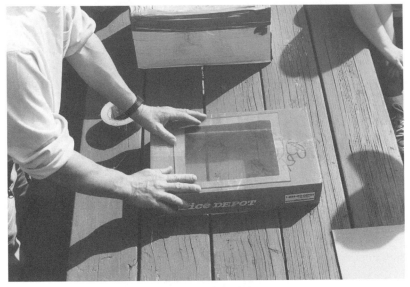

Place the pane of glass onto the top of the lid. TIMOTHY SNIDER

Securely tape the glass onto the lid.
TIMOTHY SNIDER

The low-cost but effective solar oven is now done. TIMOTHY SNIDER

that might be a consideration if you are hiding out in a war or combat situation.

If you don't feel confident making your own solar cooker from the description given here, you can buy a set of plans published by Solar Box Cookers International from Survival Services, P.O. Box 41834, Los Angeles, CA 90041. Solar Box Cookers International conducts educational activities worldwide to promote the use of solar cookers.

While people in the United States might regard solar cooking as a novelty, keep in mind that over half of the world's population still cooks its meals over a wood fire, and their "energy crisis" is the fact that people must walk farther and farther from village sites to find firewood. In Africa, about 85 percent of the population cooks over wood fires. Large influxes of refugees in some areas, such as 30,000 or so refugees in the Kakuma Refugee Camp in northwest Kenya, tax the wood resources beyond their ability to provide. In areas where solar cookers have been introduced, along with an educational program, significant progress has been made.

In spite of all the advantages of solar box cookers, the summer 1995 edition of *Solar Cooker Review* described some of the reasons why people are not using their solar cookers in Zimbabwe. In an area where solar box cookers have been introduced, some people did not use them because they missed the smoke from the fire and the ability of the smoke to repel insects. Some people simply wanted the warmth of a fire in their home. Others were fearful that someone might steal their food, or even poison it, if the food were left outside. In the United States, people generally use solar cookers because they want to, not because they have to.

In the aftermath of a major earthquake, however, residents would still have the ability to cook some meals without a fire.

REFRIGERATION
Think about it—of all our modern electric conveniences, refrigeration is probably the most difficult to replace if the electricity goes out or if you are in the wild.

When there was no electricity, people preserved their food in other ways. For example, they canned, or dried, or pickled. Or they stored things in a basement where it is cooler.

Daniel McPherson, a childhood school buddy, once took me to an abandoned remote cabin in the Angeles National Forest. There was no electricity, so there was no refrigerator. The builders of the cabin, however, devised good ways to heat the cabin and a natural way to keep some foods cool. They built a small box from two layers of wire, which they mounted on the cool north side of the cabin. Items that needed to stay cool were put into this wire box. The two layers of wire allowed for air circulation and also kept animals from getting in to the food.

They also had a similar screen-box that was kept a short distance upstream in the water. Such a box in the stream does not survive heavy winter rains when boulders came down the river, though it is relatively easy to construct another from heavy-gauge wire.

The African Pot in Pot Device
The need to refrigerate food to prevent spoilage is a universal need, whether or not there is electricity. In one Africa village, a local potter, Mohammed Bah Abba, found a way to keep greens and vegetables fresh longer.

He constructed a pot that fit into a larger pot. The space between the pots was filled with sand and then water. The vegetables were kept in the

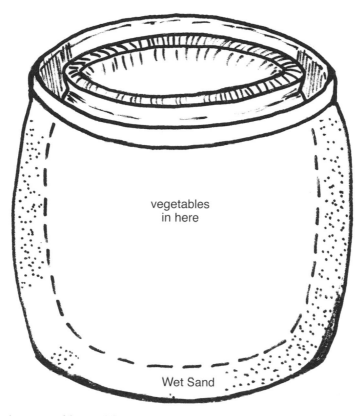

vegetables
in here

Wet Sand

Keeping vegetables and fruit longer with no electricity. A pot is placed inside a larger pot, and the space between is filled with water-saturated sand. Field tests have shown that the vegetables keep several days longer in this device than when placed in a single pot.

inner pot covered with a lid. They found that vegetables stored this way kept up to a week longer than vegetables just kept in a covered pot. Though a remarkably simple invention, the man won an award from *Time* magazine for one of the best inventions of 2001.

Chanel Patricia was a friend of ours who resided near the picturesque Arroyo Seco in Los Angeles' Highland Park district. When she remodeled her home, she had electricity, but she opted not to have a refrigerator. She insisted on living an ecological lifestyle—as much as was possible in the city—and she felt that the refrigerator was one of the largest energy users in the modern home.

How did she do without a refrigerator? For one, she refurbished the vegetable cooler that was built into most homes fifty or more years ago. This looks like a closet on the outside, but its shelves are screens. There is an opening into the basement and another opening into the attic. This allows for a flow of cool air to rise out of the basement and keep the food naturally cool.

She also disciplined herself to buy as much of her food dried or canned as possible. Lastly, she used an evaporative cooler that she devised herself, one that people in Third World countries have also devised.

She simply put her perishable items into a large dish pan with water, and everything was covered with a towel. The towel would soak up the water, and keep the food items cool. It was simple, and always a conversation item when we visited Chanel.

In some parts of the country in the pre-electricity days, ice would be cut from lakes and carted off to heavily insulated barns. My father remembers this from his childhood in rural Ohio, and it is an idea that may still be viable today.

John Watkins of Harbor City, California, once explained how he accidentally made ice in the body of the small boat he had parked in his driveway. He researched the phenomenon, and managed to repeat the process. Watkins also shared this discovery with a group of Mensans who attended a discussion at his home. Watkins told me that the members of the high IQ society believed his story was some sort of practical joke.

According to Watkins, ice can form naturally, even with night temperatures as warm as sixty degrees, by the process of differential radiation. It must be a noncloudy night for this to work. South American Indians have produced ice by this method using bales of hay and water in terra-cotta containers. Watkins explained how it could be done in one's backyard, either as a science experiment or because ice is needed.

Approximately ten bales of hay are required, so this method may not be readily viable unless you keep horses or goats. The bales are arranged so that there is an opening in their middle. The entire stack is covered in a large sheet of plastic. Into the hole in the middle, place a Styrofoam food container (the type used for ice or camping food). Fill the container about one-third full of water.

If everything is right, you will have ice in the morning.

For those who desire to live off the grid, or to prepare for periods of no electricity, consider purchasing the refrigerators that operate on twelve volts, and can be powered directly from a solar panel. There is a single unit refrigerator that is sold by some solar companies that has a solar panel in the roof. It obviously does not generate cold at night, since there is no battery pack, but the cold is generally less essential at night.

To build your own such system, purchase the largest twelve-volt refrigerator you can afford. The best source for such a refrigerator is an RV supply store. Any electrician worth his salt should be able to advise you on the size of the photovoltaic panel to buy for your refrigerator, and should also be able to wire it up for you.

HEATING WATER

Whether you're lost in the woods, living in a remote cabin, or living in the backyard after a major urban earthquake, you'll want a way to heat water. This will be for basic hygiene, to purify the water, to wash wounds, to sterilize utensils, and so forth.

If you have the ability to make a fire and you have a can, you can heat water.

But what about more challenging situations where you don't have the basics?

We've all heard of "thinking outside the box," right? So, to provide your hot water in a survival situation, think like a hobo, a farmer, or a homesteader. Fire, of course, is your first choice.

If you're in the backyard with the urban chaos all around you, but no gas or electricity to your water heater, there is still a way to heat that water. Ideally, you thought ahead and you obtained a discarded gas water heater sometime earlier, and you used it to store water. Or you just put it into the garage, intending to use it.

Take that old gas water heater—it must not have leaks—and carefully prop it up in a safe part of the yard. You'll need to get water into it— maybe with a hose if you have running water, or with a bucket and funnel. Next, build a fire underneath the water heater. Gas water heater tanks have that central smokestack, which is ideal for a little fire underneath. To get the hot water out, you can either open the drain (not the best idea, because all the hot water is up top, and because lots of sediment collects near the drain outlet) or you can force the hot water out by pressure, just as it would come out when properly installed. But if you have no water under pressure, you may have to settle for getting the water out from the drain.

I once had a backwoods shower built from an old water heater tank, with the water being heated by the sun. I began with a discarded gas water heater tank. I removed the outer shell and insulation, and I spray-painted the outside black. I cleaned out the tank from the years of built-up sediment. I carefully set the tank on top of a fifty-five-gallon drum and filled the water heater with water from the hose (yes, I had hose water, but I could have also filled the tank bucket by bucket with stream water).

The water tank was secured with a few two-by-fours so there was no chance that it would fall over and hurt someone.

After the whole day of sitting out in the sun, the water in the forty-gallon tank got pretty hot. I never measured the temperature, but it was hot enough for a good hot bath. I had an old bathtub ten feet away; I attached a hose to the water tank's drain and let the hot water drain into the tub. This was always a summer nighttime bath. It was pleasant and very refreshing after a hard day's work.

You can also produce hot water by heating it inside a solar oven.

Other variations would be to fill a brown beer bottle and set it in the sun. Obviously, you must clean the bottle first. Liquid inside a dark glass container will heat quicker than inside a clear glass container.

There are also the solar shower bags sold at backpacking stores. I have several of these and have used them enough times to realize they are definitely viable ways to have hot showers in the urban backyard, or deep in the backcountry.

You simply fill them with water, lay them in the sun for a few hours, then hang the bag up somewhere and open the spigot to take a solar-heated shower.

I once visited a remote and abandoned cabin in the Angeles National Forest. Whoever built it did a good job of planning. In the corner of the kitchen was a twenty-five-gallon water tank. Water entered the tank through conventional piping, fed by pressure upstream. But before the water entered the tank, it zigzagged in the adjacent wood stove. The wood stove wasn't a cast-iron stove, but rather a cement and cinder block stove built into the kitchen. The top was cast iron, with the look of an old wood-stove. It is possible that the top was taken from a cast-iron stove and used in the cabin.

In order to get hot water, you had to either do some cooking on the stove or simply add a few logs and let the water in the pipes heat up. Then, when you turned on the hot water spigot, hot water flowed out! It was a very low-tech way to get hot water. It was clearly an example of survival with style.

3

Health and Hygiene

There is a lot that urban dwellers take for granted. We assume that there will always be hot running water in the home, a convenient bathroom, the ready availability of medicines at the local pharmacy, and the weekly trash pickup to remove all those things we don't know how to deal with, or don't choose to.

The backpacker into the wilderness knows that all of his or her needs will be met with whatever is in the pack, or by one's wits. Backpackers carry their food and medicine or have learned how to use certain wild plants. They know that they will bathe by swimming or other simple and primitive means. Their bathroom is an outhouse or a hole dug with a shovel. They know that they must deal with all their own trash. What can't be burned or buried is carried out to somewhere else.

First-time backpackers might have a bit of adjusting to do as they get used to taking nothing for granted. In time, they learn to handle all their needs. Those who repeat the backpacking adventure discover that an inner strength is developed by forcing yourself to deal with your own needs. But this feeling of inner strength does not always come easily. It is earned by choosing to put yourself into a situation where your limits are tested. In fact, there are many people who are so challenged by this outdoor experience that they cut short their trips and head back home, vowing to never repeat such a miserable experience.

Imagine, then, the shock experienced by city dwellers who are suddenly forced to rely on their own resources. Maybe a major earthquake suddenly leveled their home, and now they have to find another home. The first few days and weeks can be a shock without electricity, probably no indoor plumbing and bathroom, none of the conveniences that we've come to expect.

Or perhaps a change in the political situation means you must grab whatever belongings you can and run to the hills.

During the first Gulf War ("Desert Storm"), this is what happened to the Kurds under Saddam Hussein, and it was winter in the hills. Or possibly a tsunami suddenly wipes out everyone and everything familiar, and you have to not only survive but figure out what to do next. This happened to over 200,000 people in December 2004. Or a major hurricane—such as Katrina, which wiped out New Orleans as the water rose—hits. Or possibly the rising tensions of war could unleash a nuclear bomb. Though we know countless Japanese disappeared in Hiroshima and Nagasaki in the bombs that ended the war, we forget that countless more who lived on the fringes survived. They survived, and suddenly they were forced to start life from scratch. Their day to day bodily needs and functions did not stop just because the bombs destroyed the infrastructure of their lives.

The possible threats to a normal living of one's life are enormous. War, tribal and interracial warfare, acts of terrorism, biological warfare, poisoning the water supply, economic manipulation and monopolies are some of the things that man does to man. Then there is nature: drought, floods, earthquakes, wildfires, hurricanes, landslides, tsunamis, sinkholes, cold spells, ice ages, comets hitting the earth, and so on. We seem to have little control over most of these natural disasters. In some cases, our actions exacerbate such disasters.

So how do we carry on in the aftermath of a major urban disaster, or of getting lost in the woods?

Let's start with the most pressing issues, and then work our way to those issues that are important, but not immediately pressing.

GOING TO THE BATHROOM

IN THE WOODS

We all have to deal with this basic biological function, maybe several times a day. Considering the fact that we know this is a regular function of everyone's body, plan ahead on how you will deal with this. Don't "wait for the last minute."

Carry a little trowel in your pack. If you didn't carry toilet paper, collect leaves that are suitable—and (all kidding aside) be sure you know how to identify poison oak and poison ivy. If you are by yourself, dig a small hole in a private spot, squat, do your thing, and then bury it back up.

When camping in a group where there is no outhouse, find a private spot that is not along any trails. We have set up group toilets where we first dug a trench approximately three feet deep. We then secured a horizontal wooden post along the length of the trench for the convenience of sitting. Toilet paper (or leaves) are kept nearby, as is a shovel. It is each person's responsibility to toss soil into the trench after each usage.

We have gone on desert trips where we drove to a remote site where there were no tables, no outhouses, no running water, no shelter or facilities of any sort—just open desert and very few trees. At one of the spots we have frequented regularly for desert survival training classes, we set to work building an outhouse as our first priority. We have constructed private outhouses out of plywood that we brought along for that purpose, with a porta potty inside. It might take about an hour to construct a temporary outhouse, one that will not fall over in the desert winds, but which can be taken apart quickly before we depart.

We have also simply dug holes under hospital toilet chairs, and then built the plywood outhouse around these chairs. After each use, one tosses a shovelful of soil into the hole.

Where plywood is unavailable, simple outhouse frames can be constructed using two-by-fours or straight branches tied together. The framework is covered with sheets of cloth or plastic (for privacy), or whatever is locally available.

Do not overlook constructing a sanitary and private outhouse, whether out camping in the backwoods or camping in the backyard. Number one, we need to evacuate regularly for optimum health. If there is no private place to "go to the bathroom," people will tend to "hold it," which is definitely not healthful. Secondly, feces and urine (and other bodily discharges) will attract flies and various vermin if left open or improperly buried. That can lead to the introduction of other sicknesses, possibly spread by flies or mosquitoes. You don't want to exacerbate an already bad situation.

Still, this should be a warning to the wise, since in most of the disasters that regularly strike someone, somewhere (earthquakes, floods, hurricanes, and so forth), the post-disaster disease often causes more deaths than the incident itself. This is because open sources of water quickly become polluted with feces, dead bodies (human and animal), and rotting vegetation.

It's important to deal with basic sanitation and deal with it forthrightly.

IN THE BACKYARD

If you have a porta potty for camping—sometimes for RVs—then you already have a toilet you can use in the aftermath of an urban disaster where the functionality of your home is gone. Or you may have a potty seat—the type that is used in hospitals. You often see these at yard and estate sales.

Set up one in a private place. Then bury the contents in a trench when full, and cover the trench with several inches of soil.

One issue will be odors and flies. There is a chemical that you can buy for use with the porta potties. Or you can use the old standby—lime. This is purchased at garden supply stores, since it is also used on lawns. No lime? Use baking soda. Baking soda (sodium bicarbonate) is one of those products that you should always have around the house, as it has hundreds of practical uses. No baking soda? Use ashes from the fire pit. After all, if you're going to be living in the backyard, you're very likely going to be cooking in some sort of improvised metal can stove or in an open fire pit. You will have plenty of ash.

For approximately a year and a half (1977–1979), I was a squatter at an old house in Los Angeles. I fixed the place up, did gardening, recycled the household water into the yard, and raised some ducks. Among other things, I experimented with a porta potty. The purpose of the experiment was to see how well we'd do with such a toilet if in the aftermath of a major earthquake, we'd have no choice but to use such a bucket toilet.

For three months, the three of us who lived in the house, as well as all guests, used the porta potty—nothing more than a plastic seat over a large bucket with a lid. We experimented with lemon juice and baking soda as an additive and found that the lemon worked quite well.

When full, the bucket was emptied into a large trench that we'd dug for that purpose. It was about four feet long, about two feet wide, and it began about three feet deep. We'd empty the contents of the bucket into the trench and add a layer of soil. When the trench was full, we planted tomato plants in the trench and got some really excellent tomatoes.

Aside from some mild odors, and the inconvenience of having to empty the bucket about once weekly, it was not that difficult to switch to such a toilet. If we'd had no other choice, it was a routine that any household could adopt easily.

Worm Toilet

Another option is the worm toilet. This consists of a hospital toilet with no bucket. Instead, a wooden box with no bottom is placed under the seat. The three toilets like this that I have experimented with were all located outside in private spots.

After each use of the toilet, you scoop in a shovelful of soil and wormy compost. This, of course, assumes you also have a worm farm in your backyard.

Though there are countless ways to make a worm farm, we have always opted for the easiest method. Ours has been a simple rectangular enclosure made of railroad ties or cinder blocks. Into this area, we put all kitchen scraps (those we cannot feed to the animals) and such small things as leaves and grass clippings. We introduce earthworms into this container. We have always used redworms, because they reproduce rapidly, have a greater temperature tolerance, and are top feeders. There are bigger earthworms, but they tend to be bottom feeders, with slow to no reproduction when in such boxes or enclosures, and they will die if it gets too hot, too cold, too wet. Redworms have always made the most sense.

Next to the outside toilet, I kept a little trowel with a bucket of wormy compost. After each use, a few trowelfuls of the wormy compost—with worms, of course—was tossed into the box enclosure. When the bottomless box was full, I would move the hospital toilet set to a new location with a new bottomless box and start all over.

I found that the worms worked to decompose the feces and toilet paper in record time, and it all had the look of fine garden soil in less than two months after the usage of each box had ceased. There were never flies around this toilet, and there were no noticeable odors.

Although our focus here is how you can have a sanitary toilet in the aftermath of an emergency, you need to be aware of where you should, and should not, use the resultant fertilizer in your yard and garden. Human-based fertilizer is fine under any ornamental shrubs and trees, and under fruit trees. More caution should be taken when used for crops whose fruit you harvest, such as tomatoes, squash, corn, and the like, though various research indicates that such fertilizer is generally safe with such vegetables where you're not using fruits or parts of the plant that come in direct contact with the soil. In general, any pathogens in the feces will have "broken down" in about two months. Thus, it is not advised to use human fertilizer on root crops (potatoes, turnips, jerusalem artichokes, horseradish, gobo, and so forth), nor is it advised on low-growing greens (spinach, mustard, collards, and the like).

IN THE TREES

I spoke with Jerry O'Dell, who—along with John Quigley—received nation-wide media attention in late 2002–2003 when they sat in an old oak tree for seventy days. The oak tree—named "Old Glory"—was in the path where housing developers wanted to put a road. O'Dell was in the tree for about seventy days from November 2002 into the first week of January. At times, there were dozens to hundreds of community activists on the ground who did not want the tree to be cut down.

I was curious—what did the tree sitters do for a toilet? They used a five-gallon bucket with a toilet seat over it. They put compost and mulch in the bottom of the bucket, and after each use they added wood ash and more mulch. In general, the bucket was lowered down each day and others disposed of the contents. O'Dell said that there was never any odor, nor flies, while using this method. This was not intended as a long-term toilet, since it was emptied daily. Still, this experience provides useful clues for anyone needing a similar convenient and simple toilet.

A FEW WORDS ABOUT URINE

In the original *Flight of the Phoenix* movie, the men whose plane crashed in the desert saved their urine and distilled it into potable water. Though this may seem unsavory at first, water can be distilled from urine through any method of distillation.

The chapter about water described how to make the desert solar still (see page 15). In high desert experiments, we poured urine into one of these stills and extracted drinkable water. It is something to keep in mind.

Some years ago, I met a man who lived at an early Israeli kibbutz. He said that they were engaged in farming, and that conditions were somewhat primitive. Water was always in short supply, and he described drinking camel urine. He said it was palatable to drink and not particularly unpleasant.

During WWII when my father Frank was stationed at an Army base in the Southern California desert, his hands became severely chapped. "They were so bad, they were bleeding," he told us. He recalled a bit of lore from his Czechoslovakian grandmother who indicated that urine was a cure for chapped skin. He went to a private spot, urinated on his hands, and found that they quickly healed. His Army buddies laughed when he told them about the experience. Frank later learned, however, that many of the men who laughed at him cured their own chapped hands with urine.

KEEPING THE BODY CLEAN

The skin is the body's largest organ. Huh? you say. Yes, our body is covered and sealed in a remarkable material that "holds it all together," and is designed to breathe, excrete poisons, and even contract and expand to help us deal with both the cold and heat. It is that excreting part that most of us don't recognize—until it is too late. And the billion dollar industries designed to keep our skin "soft and smelling good" are a part of the problem, because they sell us perfumes and oils and other questionable products that keep all those toxins trapped within the pores of our skin. Part of good vibrant health is to have clean and open pores. This is how our bodies work, and your body doesn't differentiate between being in the wilderness or city, nor does it differentiate between "normal times" and times of crisis. You skin must breathe, period.

DRY BRUSH SHOWER

Even if you have no water, it is imperative to keep the pores of the skin clean, open, and breathing for optimum health. Things such as appearance and odor are less relevant issues in a survival situation. With or without water, a brush is essential. Fortunately, if you are without a commercial brush, one can be manufactured from common materials with a little practice. (See the comments in the following section about how to make a brush.)

Take your brush to a private spot, remove your clothes, and brush everywhere. Brush steadily in each area and you'll feel your skin tingle. You'll be loosening up and removing dead skin cells that always form on the outer layer of our skin. Do your entire body this way, especially areas that itch. Itching is often a sign of a buildup of toxin or a sign of toxins being removed from the body. Brush and scrub those itchy areas well.

A thorough brush bath can be done quickly in five minutes, but you should take even more time and do it well.

Brushes from Nature
We all rely on simply brushes (and combs) for hygiene purposes: brushing our teeth, brushing our hair (which also removes dirt, insects, and ticks),

Timothy Snider examines a yucca plant.

and brushing our skin for cleanliness. Even if we've closely examined any of the various brushes in the department stores, how many of us would know how to produce a brush if suddenly we had to rely upon nature to serve this need?

Here is how you make a brush using yucca, which is common in the Western and Southwestern United States. (If you do not have yucca, find other suitable fibrous materials.)

1. Collect a handful of yucca leaves twice as long as your intended brush. They don't all have to be exactly the same length, as you can trim them when you are finished.

Geoff Angle ties a bundle of yucca leaves in order to produce a simple brush.
DUDE McLEAN

*Geoff Angle folds
down one side of
the yucca bundle
onto the other side.*
DUDE McLEAN

2. Tie the bundle tightly and securely in its middle.
3. Fold one side down over the other, layer by layer. Do this carefully so you have even layers folder over.
4. Finally, secure the bundle tightly with another cord. (In Mexico, a small wire is used.)

Note: You can make this brush with many variations. If the yucca bristles are kept stiff, you can use it as a hairbrush. If you add a handle, you have a small whisk broom. If you soften the ends of the bristles (with a rock), you have a good brush for scrubbing your skin. If it is made very small, you have a suitable toothbrush.

*Once the end
is tied off, the
brush is done.*
DUDE McLEAN

A selection of handmade yucca brushes. The brush on the lower right is made from roots, and tied off with wire; it is commonly found in Mexican markets.

Natural grooming materials. A comb made from a gourd sits on a wash cloth made from agave fiber. At top left is a rough stone that is used for cleaning pine tar from skin. On right are two dried, wild cucumbers used as luffas.

A view of the dried, wild cucumber used as you'd use a luffa.

SUN BATH

The rays of the sun are a known purifier. We also know that that body converts sunlight into vitamin D. This process occurs best if the skin is clean and the pores unclogged.

You can take a sun bath after you have done a dry brush shower or you can take one whenever you feel the need.

Find a private spot, remove your clothes, and lie down in a spot where you can get full exposure. Expose both your front and your back to the sun. You're not interested in getting a tan by doing this—just approximately five to ten minutes per side, depending on the intensity of the sun.

SOLAR HOT WATER SHOWER

If you have water in your wilderness or urban survival situation, you should use some for cleansing the body, if you can spare it. Obviously, when water is in short supply, the first priority is for the hydration of the

*Dolores Lynn
Nyerges shows the
sun shower.*

people and animals. And used water should not just be tossed out randomly, but used to water plants.

Hot water is better than cold water for cleansing. If you have a fire, it should be a simple matter to find a large pot to heat the water.

If you can't have a fire, you can also heat your wash water in the sun by any of several simple methods. Several manufacturers have produced the simple sun shower, which is a sturdy bag with a sturdy handle and a spigot. These are definitely worth buying. I have used them on numerous occasions. My only complaint is that on occasion the water was *too* hot! You fill these with water, lay them in the sun, and in anywhere from one to three hours, you hang it in a tree and take a hot shower.

I have also made a make-shift sun shower by adding some surgical tubing to a plastic water container. The surgical tubing was added to the spout, and the tubing was simply folded back to stop the water flow. I would set these in the sun, and though less portable than their commercial counterpart, they definitely heated water.

Other simple ways to heat water with the sun:

1. Remove the outer shell and insulation from a discarded gas water heater. (It must still hold water.) The water tank should already be black. If not, spray it black. Make sure the clean-out valve is functioning—these typically fill with sediment and do not work well. You may need to remove the existing valve, clean out the bottom of the tank, and add a new spigot. I set mine out in the sun on top of a fifty-five-gallon drum. I need the height of the drum, because I took my shower by letting the water drain from this water tank. Fill the tank with water from a garden hose or hand fill it with a funnel. This will be heavy, so be sure to set it where you want it to be. After a few hours in the sun, you will be able to stand under the drain valve, and open it to take a warm to hot shower.

   In one past residence, I did this so that the water drained into an outside bathtub, and I took many very pleasant evening baths in the yard.

2. A large black plastic trash bag can be filled with water and set out in a sunny place. The water will be hot in an hour or more. This can be a bit unwieldly, but it does heat the water.

3. A large can, painted black on the outside, set in the sun and covered with a sheet of plastic, will also work.

An old gas water heater tank has been stripped of its shell, and is now used as a solar water heater.

NATURE'S SOAPS

The chart on page 98 shows just some of the common wild soaps found in nature. There are soap plants found everywhere, and most can be prepared very simply.

When anthropologists start talking about man's change from nomadic to a settled lifestyle, they bring up key factors like domestication of crops and animals, and permanent housing. We domesticated ourselves and became less wild. And right there from the beginning, there was soap. There had to be. Think about it—men and women living together in the same permanent dwelling *without* soap? Soap had to be there. When soap wasn't there, the men got thrown out. Soap not only helped people get along, but it also kept them healthier.

Today, we've gotten so civilized that we long to get back into nature, to fill our backpacks and go rough it for a weekend or longer. But we're so civilized that we've totally forgotten that "soap" is abundant in nature. Most of these soap plants were used by Native Americans, and some are considered ornamentals. In fact, there are quite a few plants that contain saponins, though not in volumes that make the plants useful as soap.

Soap plants are quite a bit different from the "old-fashioned" soap that grandma used to make on the farm—those hard bars of soap we associate with the pioneer days. Most of those soaps were made from a combination of animal fats (pig, cow) and lye (processed from wood ashes in the old days). That's not what I'm talking about here. If you wish to make homemade bars of soaps, there are numerous good books that tell you everything you need to know.

Let's examine a few of the common wild soap plants.

Amole

There is the fairly widespread member of the lily family with the tennis ball size bulb referred to as amole *(Chlorogalum pomeridianum)*. The long

Nyerges makes soap with an amole root. TIMOTHY SNIDER

A COMPARISON OF WILD SOAP PLANTS

	Part Used	Process	Ease of Collection	Where Found
Amole *Chlorogalum pomeridianum*	Bulbous root	Agitate fresh, crushed root between hands with water	Difficult in hard soil, since root may be a foot deep	Widespread in areas but extremely difficult to locate when dormant
Bouncing Bet *Saponaria officinalis*	Leaves	Agitate fresh leaves between hands with water	Simply snip leaves	Generally a garden plant; often escaped
Buffalo Gourd *Cucurbita foetidissima*	Leaves	Agitate tender leaves between hands with water	Simply snip leaves	Common and widespread in parts of Southwest
Mountain Lilac *Ceanothus* spp.	Flowers and fruits	Agitate fresh flowers or fresh or dried fruits between hands with water	Easy to collect flowers and fruits, though trees are often in difficult terrain	Common and widespread throughout Southwest
Soaproot *Chenopodium californicum*	Taproot	Grate fresh or dried root, agitate between hands with water	Difficult in hard soil; a shovel may be required	Found in scattered isolated patches; somewhat difficult to find
Yucca *Yucca* spp.	Leaves	Strip fresh leaf into fibers, agitate between hands with water	A sharp knife or pair of clippers is required to cut the tough leaf	Extremely common and widespread

linear leaves measure a foot and longer, and they are wavy on their margins. When you dig down—sometimes up to a foot deep in hard soil—you'll find the bulb, which is entirely covered in layers of brown fibers. I have seen useful brushes and whisk brooms made from a cluster of these fibers that had been gathered and securely wrapped on one end with some cordage.

Availability	Lather	Cleansing Ability	Cautions	Comments
Bulbs can be used year-round	Rich, thick lather with an almost oily quality	Excellent cleaning properties		A top quality soap, though not as easy to find as others
Leaves can be used year-round if no snow	Medium to low lather	Acceptable		Worth planting in your yard as a "useful orna-mental"
Leaves generally unavailable in late summer and fall	Medium to low lather, depending on leaf moisture content	Acceptable	Stiff hairs on leaf may cause irrita-tion to skin	Use when no other soap plants are available
Flowers and fruits available only in spring; fruits can be dried for year-round use	Medium to rich lather with very mild sweet aroma	Good	Dried seeds might irritate hands when making soap; grind into powder first	A fragrant, pleas-ant soap to use when in season
Root can be dug year-round, though it's hard to locate when dormant; root can be dried and stored	Extremely rich, thick lather	Very good		Arguably "the best" wild soap, though not widely available
Leaves available year-round	Low to medium to rich lather, depending on species	Extremely good cleansing properties; leaf fiber aids in cleansing	The leaf tip and edges are extremely sharp, so be careful when gathering	Because yucca is widespread, available year-round, and makes a good soap, I use it the most

For the soap, you remove the brown fiber until you have the white bulb. It is formed in layers, just like an onion, and you'll find it sticky and soapy to the touch. Take a few layers of the white bulbs, add water, and agitate them between your hands. A rich lather results, which you can use to take a bath, wash your hair, wash your clothes, or clean your dog.

The bulbs can be dug year-round if you know where to dig; when the plant is dormant in late fall and winter, there is only scant evidence to tell you that the bulbs are underground. Though the bulbs can be dug and dried for future use, the fresh bulb is superior.

Bouncing Bet

Bouncing bet *(Saponaria officinalis)*, also known as soapwort, is widespread. It is commonly planted as a garden plant for its pink flowers and occurs wild in some areas. It is an introduced plant with little history of use by Native Americans.

The leaves or the roots can be used, though I prefer to use the leaves simply because once you pull the root, the plant is gone. Bouncing bet is made into soap by agitating the fresh leaves between your hands with water. The quality of lather varies, but it is worth knowing about should the plant grow abundantly in your area.

Bouncing bet in bloom.

Buffalo gourd.

Buffalo Gourd

Buffalo gourd *(Cucurbita foetidissima)* is widely spread throughout the Southwestern United States, and can be found in remote deserts and in urban vacant lots. It also goes by such local names as coyote melon and calabazilla. This is an obvious relative of squash and pumpkins. The small orange-shaped gourds have been used as rattles by Southwestern Indians, though they make a somewhat inferior rattle. The wandering vine arises from a huge underground root, and the stiff leaves often stand upright. They have a unique aroma, and the leaves are covered with tiny rigid spines.

To make soap, pinch off a handful of the tender growing tips or just the older leaves if that's all you can find. Add water and agitate the tips or leaves between your hands. A green frothy lather results, which was used for washing clothes by Southwestern tribes. Buffalo gourd, however, is regarded by some as the soap of last resort since the tiny hairs may irritate the skin.

*Two hikers look
at the mountain
lilac flowers.*

Mountain Lilac

Mountain lilac (*Ceanothus* spp.) is a shrub to a small tree that is fairly common throughout the West. Various species of *Ceanothus* are found throughout the United States. When you are hiking through chaparral, desert, or mountain regions in the spring, you will notice a spot of the white or blue flowers on the hillside or along the trail. There are many species that you can use for soap, and they also go by the names of buckbrush, snowbrush, and soapbloom. Since the botanical features of each species vary, the easiest way to determine if you have a mountain lilac is to take a handful of blossoms, add water, and rub them between your hands. You'll get a good lather with a mild aroma if you have mountain lilac.

By late spring to early summer, the flowers fall off and the tiny sticky green fruits develop. These too can be rubbed between the hands with water to make a good soap. The fruits can also be dried and then reconstituted later when soap is needed. I tried making soap with fruits that I had dried five years earlier. The fruits were very hard, so I first ground them up in my mortar and pestle. Then I added water, rubbed vigorously, and had soap. Not as good as from the fresh fruit, but soap nevertheless.

Soaproot
One of the more interesting wild soaps is found in a genus of mostly edible and medicinal plants. Soaproot *(Chenopodium californicum)* is related to the nutritious lamb's-quarter *(C. album)*, the quinoa *(C. quinoa)*, and epazote *(C. ambrosioides)*. In fact, you could cook the leaves of soaproot, change the water, and serve it as you would spinach. Most people looking at soaproot for the first time would think it was a type of lamb's-quarter, but if they were observant, they'd know that something was different.

Timothy Snider examines the soaproot's root, which produces a great lather.

Timothy Snider examines the soaproot plant's leaf.

For one thing, soaproot has a large taproot, with a shape similar to a carrot or a large ginseng root. In hard soil, the root can be a foot deep and you'll need a good digging stick or a shovel to reach it.

To make soap, you first grate the root. Grate with your knife or a kitchen grater. Then add water and rub the grated root between the hands to get a top quality, thick lather. It's a remarkable experience to produce that frothy lather from this plant. In most cases, it seems superior to even store-bought soaps, and it cleans quite well.

Native peoples often dried and stored this root for later use. When dry, it seems like a rock or a piece of hardwood. Yet, once grated, you can still get a top quality soap by adding water.

Unfortunately, soaproot seems to be found in scattered locations. It is possible that urban sprawl has destroyed much of this since it grows from its perennial root. I have never found large patches of soaproot, but only isolated patches. You should, therefore, only use small taproots and leave the rest. I also take the seeds in summer and scatter them widely so more plants will grow. If you don't plan to take these precautions, I would suggest you leave this one alone entirely.

Yucca

There are numerous species of yucca found widely, mostly throughout the Plains and Western states. They resemble big pincushions, with their long,

Christopher Nyerges shreds a yucca leaf.
TIMOTHY SNIDER

Christopher Nyerges wets the shredded yucca leaf, agitates between hands, and produces a quality soap.
TIMOTHY SNIDER

linear, needle-tipped leaves. In fact, yucca can truly be called the "grocery store" or the "hardware store" of the wild since this plant produces not only soap, but several good foods, tinder, top-quality fiber, sewing needles, and carrying cases or quivers from the mature, hollowed-out flower stalks.

Though the use of the root has been widely popularized, I have found that you need only cut one leaf to make soap. The job of digging up one yucca plant is considerable (not to mention possible legal ramifications), and to kill off a yucca just to wash your hands hardly seems justifiable. Besides, the soap from the leaf is perhaps 10 to 20 percent inferior to the soap from the root, but you get this leaf soap at perhaps 5 percent of the labor needed to dig up a root. So leave the roots alone. When you need soap, carefully cut off one leaf. Be very careful not to poke yourself with one of the sharp tips and not to slice your fingers on the very sharp edges of the leaf. To remove just one leaf, I have found that garden hand clippers work well, as do the scissors of my Swiss Army knife. First, snip off the sharp tip so you don't poke yourself. Then strip the leaf into fibers until you have a handful of very thin strands. Last, add water, agitate the strands between your hands, and you have a good quality soap.

Typically, I show my students how to twine rope or weave cord from the yucca fibers. We make a length of about two feet and then once everyone makes green soap, I tell them that they have nature's very own "Irish soap-on-a-rope." The rope is the soap, and one strand lasts about a weekend when you're in the wilds.

Alma uses yucca leaf soap to wash Jay's hair.

Overall, yucca soap is the one I have used most often and in the most diverse of circumstances because the plant is widespread, easy to recognize, and is generally available for picking year-round.

Soap is one of the many things we take for granted in our modern society. Most of use wouldn't have a clue how to make soap if suddenly we didn't have stores to go to. Fortunately in this case, nature provides us with many ready-to-use soaps. There is never an excuse to stay stinky and dirty in the outdoors. Soaps are everywhere!

KEEPING YOUR CLOTHES FRESH

Try to have at least one change of clothes. In a survival situation, the ability to change garments helps provide a tremendous feeling of well-being. *(Also see the comments about clothing in chapter four.)*

If at all possible, wash your garments regularly. Let them dry while you wear the other set of clothes. I once experienced a time when even this was not possible, and I would wash the clothes I had, wring them out as best I could, and put them right back on, letting my body heat and air temperature dry them. This was clearly not an ideal situation, but it would have been intolerable to continue wearing dirty clothes (for many reasons). It worked out well because it was summer. In winter time, such an experience may have resulted in loss of body temperature if the clothes took a long time to dry.

If it is not possible to wash your clothes regularly, you can turn them inside out and lay them in the sun. The sun disinfects and helps to freshen them up.

BRUSHING YOUR TEETH

In parts of Africa and the Middle East, there grows a tree known as peelu *(Salvador persica)*. For centuries, people would take a small pencil-sized twig, chew on the end to fray it, and then brush their teeth with it. Though the tree is not found in the United States (as far as I am aware), enterprising individuals have ground up the branches of this tree and now sell it as a popular toothpaste that is said to be particularly good for the gums.

Little twigs of both oak and willow can be used similarly. Willow is softer, though the oak is said to be a bit better for the gums. When I used to demonstrate making these simple toothbrushes during plant walks, herbalist Marge Hartwick always preferred the oak, saying that the tannic acid in the oak made it good for the teeth and gums.

Toothpaste? Baking soda is an old standard backup, possibly mixed with a little salt. In an emergency, you can use the white ash from your fire pit. Mix it with a bit of water, use as toothpaste, and rinse well.

BRUSHING YOUR HAIR

While lost in the woods, or in the aftermath of a catastrophe, keeping your hair clean is about more than appearances. The comb or brush helps remove dirt and other debris that may have accumulated in your hair, especially with longer-haired people. Brushing or combing also helps to eliminate such things as ants, spiders, fleas, and so forth.

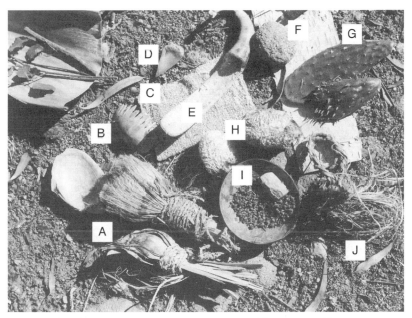

A. Yucca brushes.
B. Gourd comb.
C. Agave fiber cloth.
D. A flint knife.
E. A gourd skin scraper.

F. A rubbing stone (for tar).
G. Cactus for a hair conditioner.
H. Wild cucumber luffas.
I. Wild lilac berries for soap.
J. Shredded yucca for soap.

Keep a sturdy comb in your survival kit as they are time-consuming to manufacture. If your home was destroyed by an earthquake, you might be able to rummage around and find a good comb. But if your home was blown away in a hurricane or flooded, then you would have to learn how to make a comb.

A brush can be made with stiff yucca leaves or similar leaves, as described above. A brush for the hair should be stiffer and shorter than one used for cleaning the skin.

The comb is made by carving one from a piece of horn, or wood, or even plastic. It will take a while, and be careful to always carve away from yourself so you don't cut your fingers. To smooth out the rough parts, you should abrade the comb on a flat piece of sandstone or cement sidewalk.

DEALING WITH GARBAGE
Composting and Worm Farming
Everyone should know how to deal with garbage, especially their own. If not dealt with, you can attract flies, mosquitoes, mice, rats, roaches—all the things that can spread disease and exacerbate an already bad situation.

Since 1967, I have always used some form of a compost device for recycling all of my kitchen scraps. If I couldn't feed the scraps to the dogs, cats, chickens, rabbits, goose, ducks, pig, or other animals we may have had, it went into the compost/worm farm. This is so easy to do that it is amazing it is not more universally practiced.

In normal times, you should make the effort to set up some spot or container for making compost. If you are unfamiliar with these ideas, see *Rodale's All-New Encyclopedia of Organic Gardening.* You will see that there are many ways to compost leaves and grass and kitchen scraps.

When leaves settle and accumulate on the forest floor, season after season, the lower layers begin to decompose. They are naturally composting. Composting is how nature recycles. You can do that too with *some* discards—coffee grounds, crushed egg shells, onion skins, and so on. But most kitchen garbage will attract flies, hornets, roaches, or rats, if simply left out in the open. And remember that after most natural disasters, health authorities remind us that the diseases that accompany a breakdown in clean water supplies and garbage disposal often result in more deaths than the disaster itself.

One way to dispose of garbage is to simply dig a hole each time you have to dispose of something, and bury it. Bury it at least a foot deep to discourage animals from digging it up.

If you are going to be in one area for a while, you should make some sort of compost pit. Every backyard in America should have their own compost pit/worm farm. You become a part of the solution to the solid waste problem that faces us all, and you will be a little less vulnerable yourself.

Though this subject is thoroughly covered in the Rodale book mentioned above, here are a few simple ways to deal with kitchen wastes.

Take a trash can with a tight-fitting lid, and cut off the bottom. Put a screen in the bottom (a discarded window screen is fine). Put the trash can somewhere on soil, and with exposure to the sun. Start tossing your kitchen scraps into the container. You can also add grass or leaves, especially in the beginning. If you add to this composter regularly, it will get hot and the contents will decompose.

You will note that the commercial composters that many cities are encouraging residents to use are very much like the makeshift one described above. If your city offers these commercial composters, get one or two and begin using them.

Another option is to simply define a rectangular area in the soil with railroad ties or building blocks, and begin adding compost to it. In the beginning, it would be good to make a cover for such a composter out of a piece of plywood or an old carpet. Just lift up the carpet or plywood when you add more garbage. A composter like this can be built small or large. The smaller ones will have all the garbage in one place and thus will get hotter and decompose quicker. A larger one may not get as hot all at once, but will afford you the option to also raise earthworms. Earthworms are good because they eat the garbage and rapidly decompose it while they also increase the nitrogen content of the soil. I prefer the larger composter, so I can continually add new ingredients, but it never gets so hot that the worms are killed off.

Again, devise *some* cogent method for dealing with waste, and communicate that method to everyone in your party or family. At the very

*The author shows
the rabbit cage
positioned over
a compost
pit/worm farm.*
RAUL CASTELLANO

least, bury all garbage and let the miracles of life turn it back into soil. Do not simply scatter garbage on the surface—you can see (and smell) around nearly every homeless camp throughout the country (in both the cities and rural areas). Garbage scattered on the surface is always an invitation to insects, diseases, and misery.

Besides all of the above, your complete health requires a good diet of nutritious foods, regular and vigorous exercise, intense breathing, and a good mental outlook (to mention but a few essentials). If your home is lost or severely damaged, your ability to do all of the above will be severely challenged.

Unfortunately, we often become antagonistic and competitive in the aftermath of a disaster. It is necessary to always remind ourselves that everyone has the same needs, that we are all in the same boat, and that we will all do better if we accept the assistance of others and also seek to provide whatever assistance we can.

4

Clothing and Shelter

CLOTHING

SUMMARY

- Clothes should be comfortable, durable, and worn for the season. What's "cool" and "in" is irrelevant.
- A hat is essential. Shoes must not be too tight, and high heels for women should be banned. As for pockets—have lots of them.
- Generally, natural fabrics are best. They are breathable and will serve you well in the broadest range of environments.

Think about it—your clothing is your shelter. It is your close-to-your-body made-of-fabric shelter that you just happen to wear close to your body. When you venture into the backcountry, you very carefully choose that close shelter based on terrain, time of year, projected weather conditions, etc. It is the shelter that is always with you. If you get separated from your pack and gear, the quality of your clothing can mean the difference between life and death.

In the urban areas, too many of us are very lax about the cloth shelters that we wear. We end up wearing inappropriate fabrics, and otherwise unsuitable garments because we want to attract attention to ourselves, or we think it will make us look "cool" (or "hot"), even though such decorative garments are almost always ill-suited to the rigors of a survival situation.

The very nature of some survival situations is that they occur unexpectedly. Of course we do not dress for that situation—that's not what we expect to happen. The car breaks down in a remote area, a terrorist bomb explodes, a major earthquake shakes, and suddenly our dinner plans are ruined. It is likely that we might be wearing whatever clothes we happen to have on for a few days at least.

Dressing for survival needn't mean that you adopt military dress, with camo vests and black boots. Nor does it mean that you have to look like an ultra-nerd. It simply means that you plan ahead what fabrics to select and which to avoid. You choose each and every garment with survival in mind.

As often is the case in such matters, what you *don't do* (or, in this case, don't buy) is probably more important than what you do buy.

One of the lessons of September 11 in New York City, as thousands of men and women ran to safely, was the utter folly of the women's high heel shoe. It is well-known that the high heel shoe is not good for the spine, makes it hard for the woman to walk due to imbalance, and squeezes the toes so that the toes have no wiggle room as obviously intended by nature.

Thousands of high heels were found on the streets of New York along the exit corridors from the Twin Towers, tossed there by women who needed to be able to run. It was better to risk scratching and cutting one's feet than it was to attempt to hobble-run in ill-suited high heels. High heels not only ruin your feet and your spine, they cripple you and render you unable to run.

FOOTWEAR

Footwear is critical to foot travel, but one need not go around all day in the city wearing boots. You could wear boots all the time in the city if you wanted, however, as many have become fashionable.

Many athletic shoes are comfortable and well-made, and would easily stand up to the rigors on a trail or in a survival situation. I often wear all-black running shoes, which seem to be ordinary office sport shoes.

Shoes should have some tread, though a large heel is not necessary. They should not be too tight and constricting to the feet. Aside from being uncomfortable, too-tight shoes mean your feet cannot be insulated well, and you will be subject to frostbite on cold nights.

"... put thy shoes upon thy feet ..." Ezekial 24:17.

Shoes should be well-constructed as well. Shoes need not be water-proof, though that's a great feature if available.

One of the problems with footwear today is that so many are "dispos-able," and fewer manufacturers make a shoe that lasts long enough to be resoled, over and over again. Shoes that can be resoled seem to have died out with the family farm. Yet, they are still out there. Some brands that can be resoled are Whites, Ecco, Danner, and Asolo. There are others too—just ask for them.

So, unless you make your own shoes, look for well-constructed shoes with as many of the ideal features as possible. Of course, purchase on sale where possible.

So far, I've been speaking of commercially manufactured footwear. But it wasn't that long ago (especially if we think in cosmic terms) that every-one went barefoot or constructed their own footwear.

Going barefoot isn't really viable in urban areas, due to the ubiquitousness of broken glass, pieces of metal, and other items that will cause discomfort and even harm. There are other issues about going barefoot also. For example, even the harmful sound waves that our bodies will experience *through our feet* in the city can be harmful. You need footwear, period.

By the way, when I first met Cody Lundin, founder of Aboriginal Living Skills School in Arizona, he was barefoot in the city. He told me he goes everywhere barefoot, unless forced to wear footwear. I was impressed. He was well-versed in the philosophy and pragmatics of going barefoot, and I am certain he learned a lot by this chosen nonattire. If you choose to also experiment along these lines, keep in mind the warnings I have given and proceed like a scientist. Monitor the results, attempt to view what is happening objectively, and keep notes. I'd love to hear about it. (*If you want to know more about Cody, contact him at* alssadverntures.com *or at Box 3064, Prescott, AZ 86302.*)

Many of the traditional sandals of the past are worthy of note.

One of the simplest sandals is made with a thick piece of leather or rawhide, to which two straps are attached at the top to secure it to the foot. Such a sandal will look like so-called flip-flops or beach walkers.

If leather or rawhide is unavailable, you can make a fairly good and serviceable pair of sandals by cutting two soles from plywood or other hardwood. The straps can be riveted into the wood, or you can tack in a broad piece of leather that goes over the top of your foot. These are quickly made and are akin to Dutch wooden shoes. Master jazz musician Juno Lewis used to make and wear his own "African shoes" just this way—a thick wooden base, over which he tacked a strip of leather.

Slightly more complicated leather sandals have been made for centuries by the Plains Indians and others. One of the best descriptions of how to make these can be found in *The Indian Tipi* by Reginald and Gladys Laubin.

Woven sandals (typically made from yucca or agave fiber) were common in the Southwest. The thick Chumash-style sandal was the equivalent of our boot. One can be made in about an hour (time includes collecting and processing raw materials). There is also the flat Mogollon sandal, also common throughout the Southwest. The best description of this style of

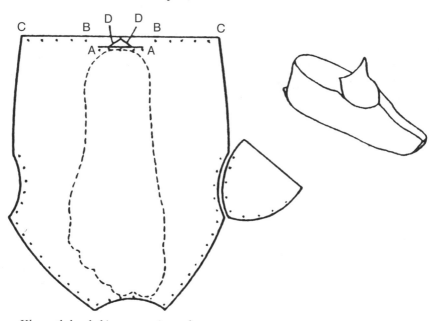

Klamath buckskin mocassin and pattern. DRAWING BY LESLIE SPIER, 1930.

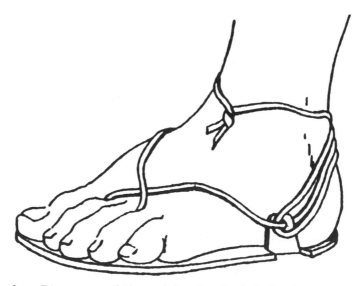

Southern Diegueno rawhide sandal and method of tying it. DRAWING BY LESLIE SPIER, 1923.

sandal can be found in Paul Campbell's *Survival Skills of Native California* (Layton, Utah: Gibbs Smith, 1999).

Socks

Wool socks are best for many reasons. They're comfortable, and they insulate better than cotton or synthetics. They also help wick moisture away from your feet. Wool wears out quickly, however, with rugged use. Wool with approximately 15 percent polyester is a good choice for the ideal blend of comfort and longevity.

Did you read *Hole in the Sky* by Pete Hautman? It's a great science fiction tale about a group of students whose survival skills were being tested on another planet. They could just as well have been on some remote island on earth. The author rather accurately noted how quickly clothes deteriorate in a survival situation, especially socks. In a long-term survival situation, the ability to fabricate your own clothes (from plants or animal skins) may be a necessary skill.

PANTS

The best pants fabrics are cotton, wool, or possibly some blend. Polyesters (with rare exceptions) are not great in the heat or in the cold. Avoid them.

Choose pants that fit well at the waist and yet have comfortable legs. Deep pockets—and many—are great choices.

In a long-term survival situation, it is likely you will lose weight. Pants with the option of adding suspenders are worth considering for this reason. Even if your pants do not have the buttons for adding suspenders, it is relatively easy to add such an option as needed, and relatively easy to braid some suspenders when needed.

Do you believe that you need camouflage pants? In the city, camo pants are counterproductive, as they tend to draw attention to you. In the wilderness, simple khaki pants are fine. You can blend into most environments with khaki in order to hide from people or animals. Camo is not necessary for most animals, since wild animals generally don't have great eyesight. Animals detect you with their sense of smell and hearing.

The camo design might be OK for some military applications, but in the urban setting they have very little camouflage value. They are more about impressing your friends and have limited survival value.

A COMPARISON OF COMMON CLOTHING FABRICS

		Insulating quality	Longevity
Animal[2]	Sheep Wool	Its hollow follicles trap air, and thus will insulate even when wet.	Due to its elasticity, there is a high wear resistance; yet in hard use, it wears out quicker than other fabrics.
	Silk	Can soak up to 30 percent of its weight in moisture and still feel dry.	High wear-resistance, but exposure to sunlight weakens.
Plant[3]	Cotton	Little to none when wet.	Poor, especially in harsh conditions; rots in sunlight, and subject to mildew.
	Linen	Slightly better than cotton.	Much better than cotton. Some linens found in tombs are thousands of years old.
MS*	Polyester	Except in special cases, no insulating value.	Excellent for longevity, which is why polyester is added to other fabrics for strength.
	Nylon		
	Acrylic		
	Modacrylic		

The left margin labels the first four rows as **NATURAL** and the last four rows as **MAN-MADE**.

[1]Tensile strength is relative, depending on the garment or fabric. However, if you attempt to tear a cord of equal thickness of the above fabrics, they will break in the following order: cotton, linen, wool, silk, polyester. The other manufactured fibers are too complex to make such simple comparisons.

Tensile strength[1]	Pro	Con	Comments
Good.	Insulates when wet, and fire-resistant, relatively wrinkle-free. Some modern wools (such as "smart wool") are outstanding.	Poor quality wool (e.g., reprocessed) is scratchy; there can be much shrinkage; can be heavy.	There are many thicknesses and qualities of wool. These produce some of your best overall "survival" garments.
A filament of silk is stronger than an equal filament of steel.	Comfortable; does not retain body odors. Lightweight, yet insulative. Fire-resistant.	Weakens with excessive sunlight; wrinkles easily.	Raw silk is probably best for all environments.
Depends on weave and thickness, but generally low.	Comfortable, inexpensive. Breathable.	Shrinks, colors run, doesn't insulate when wet.	An important historical fiber because of its comfort, ease in dying, and ease of laundering.
Quite strong and resistant to tearing. Medium.	Good in hot weather, breathable, durable. Tends not to retain body odors.	Non-insulating, so best in warm climates. Shrinks, wrinkles easily.	Historically used in hot climates due to its noninsulative but cooling properties.
Excellent, which is why polyester makes superior rope.	Long lasting; no need to iron.	No insulating value; melts when too hot.	Probably best added in small amounts to other fabrics; in some cases—such as Polartec—you have an excellent fabric that rivals wool.
			The primary raw materials are coal and petroleum. The raw materials are modified to produce different polymers and eventually different synthetic fibers.

[2]Other animal fibers: wool from goats, rabbits, alpacas
[3]Other plant fibers: ramie, hemp, kenaf, jute, sisal, etc.
*MS = Manufactured Synthetics.

A COMPARISON OF COMMON CLOTHING FABRICS continued

			Insulating quality	Longevity
M A N - M A D E	**MR****	Rayon/Viscose		
		Acetate/Triacetate		
		Tencel		

**MR = Manufactured Regenerated
NOTE: No values are given to the "manufactured" fabrics on the lower half of the chart, except polyester, because of the complexity of these fibers and the ways in which they are

SHIRTS/BLOUSES

There is nothing wrong with being fashionable, but you'd be doing yourself a favor by letting the fashion follow the function. Look for shirts and blouses with a few pockets—even button-down pockets are not unheard of on shirts.

For survival considerations, you might look for fashionable khaki-type shirts/blouses at backpacking stores. For summer use, cotton is probably best, and a bit of linen added in would improve durability.

According to Dennis Goldsmith, who created Boulevard Blouses, "Linen gets softer as it is washed. You will find that it improves with age, breaking down so that it is not as crisp and therefore wrinkles less. . . . I feel that linen works well with everything—tweeds, silks, cottons, and more linen."

Also, there are *two alternatives* to the relatively high cost of survival garments that you see at backpacking shops—the garments with all the pockets and hidden compartments and epaulets.

1. Go to thrift stores and military surplus stores and seek out the best available shirts. You'd be amazed what you can buy for just a few dollars.

2. Learn to sew. Not only is this a great skill, but it's also a possible home business. Though I am no tailor and can barely operate an

Tensile strength[1]	Pro	Con	Comments
			Fibers made wholly or mainly of regenerated cellulose. Spruce and eucalyptus are high-grade cellulose.

blended. They are shown here primarily to put them in context with the natural fibers. We would appreciate any additional hard data that helps to improve this comparative chart. Special thanks to Prudence Boczarski-Daniel who assisted with the accuracy of this chart.

electric sewing machine, I have made numerous garments using only scissors, needles, and thread. If you are just getting started, make your first garments from a lower-quality fabric. Then, when you know what you are doing, make your shirts and blouses with better quality cotton or wool.

Good wool shirts—sometimes silk lined—are incredibly comfortable and warm for winter use.

MAKE A VEST

A vest is an easy first-time sewing project. And a good vest will keep your torso warm, which is important. You can make one from an old blanket and add pockets and buttons.

Simply follow the pattern on the next page. There are only thee pieces to a vest: the back and the two sides. Make one from newspaper first, and see if it fits. When you have the size right, then you can cut and sew your blanket or other fabric.

MAKE A CAPOTE

Capotes were made by Native Americans on the Plains. Using "trade blankets," they cut and sewed these beautiful hooded capes. One capote can be

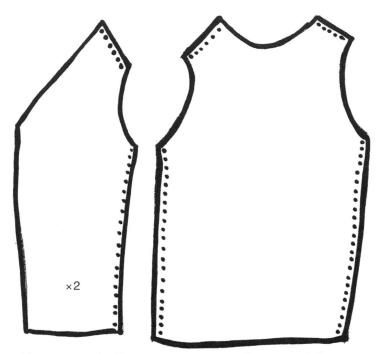

A vest is easy to make. You can trace a pattern from any existing vest or use this one. Make it out of newspaper first to make sure it will fit. Be sure to leave a little extra material where the parts are sewn together.

made from a large blanket. Again, cut one from newspaper first to make sure the size is right. Then cut and sew your blanket.

There is one piece for the body, one piece for the hood, and a piece for each arm. A separate strip is used for the belt.

The capote goes down to the knees and is very comfortable in cold weather.

If you feel unable to sew a capote from the directions provided here, you can purchase a pattern from many fabric shops.

DOUBLE THE SIZE OF YOUR WARDROBE

A cartoon from the comic pages once showed a man who declared that he had a trick for doubling the size of his wardrobe. How did he do it? "I also wear my clothes inside out," he declared.

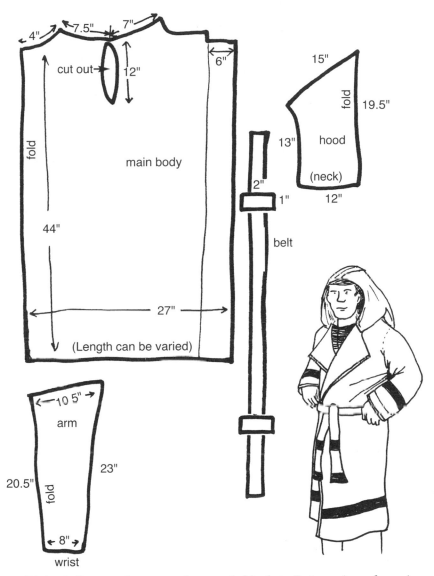

4"   7.5"   7"

cut out→   12"

15"

fold   19.5"

6"

13"   hood

fold   (neck)

main body

2"   1"   12"

44"

belt

27"

(Length can be varied)

10 5"

arm

23"

20.5"   fold

8"

wrist

Plains Indians made capotes from trade blankets. Pattern pieces for a size thirty-eight capote. Use one large wool blanket. Drawings are not to scale. Measure everything carefully before you make any cuts.

Laying out the capote pattern onto a blanket.
DOLORES LYNN
NYERGES

All kidding aside, clothes wear out in certain spots of constant stress and impact. Elbows, knees, heels, the seat—these are places that tend to go first and then the garment must be repaired. In a survival situation where you cannot readily get replacement garments (a war situation, serious economic hard times, homelessness), you will want your clothes to last longer.

In fact, by wearing the garments inside out, you will be stressing the fabric in a different way. It may not actually double the life of the garment, but it will certainly extend its useful life. Also, in addition to wearing them inside out, you can wear them backwards. This means there are actually four ways you can wear a given garment, in most cases. In a genuine survival situation, you are not concerned about fashion. Nor are you concerned about making a good first impression.

The author tries on a newly made capote. DOLORES LYNN NYERGES

POST–WORLD WAR II LESSON

In 1972, two residents of the village of Talofofo in the southern part of Guam were out hunting along the river when they heard a sound in the tall reeds. At first they thought it was an animal or a small child, but out of the bushes came a wild-appearing Japanese man carrying a shrimp trap. The hunters were startled at first, and after a few confused words, the hunters subdued the man and took him back to their corrugated metal home in the jungle.

The police were summoned, and eventually the saga of Shoichi Yokoi became known to the world. He was a sergeant in the Japanese Army who hid out in a cave during WWII, refusing to surrender. He learned in 1952 that the war was over, from a leaflet that he found in the jungle. "We Japanese soldiers were told to prefer death to the disgrace of getting

*Jon Sherman tests
a plastic trash bag
as a raincoat.*

captured alive," he said. Originally there were nine men in the cave. Eight years before he was captured, there were just three men left, then the other two died. His story was well-documented in books and magazine articles.

As you know, clothing does not last. The reporters who saw Yokoi's clothing after his capture were amazed. They could not determine what sort of material it was made from. He had been a tailor before the war and knew how to sew. He beat the bark of the pago tree into flat pieces of fabric that resembled burlap bags, and sewed them together to make a total of three "suits" (three pairs of pants and three shirts) during his twenty-eight years on the island. He beat pieces of brass to create his sewing needle, and made thread from the pago tree bark. His shirts had outside pockets for carrying things, his pants had belt loops, and he even made buttons from the plastic of an old flashlight.

It turned out that Yokoi had "rediscovered" one of the secrets of Guam's past—the making of a rough cloth from the pago fiber.

BELTS
Though this applies to men's more than women's dress, many women's outfits are suitable for the belt. Though the obvious function of the belt is to hold up our pants, pants that fit well need no belt.

If I had a choice of pants with an elastic waistband, or one with belt loops, I'd always choose the belt loops. A belt serves many possible uses. You can hang things on your belt—keys, knife, little pack, fire starter, canteen, gloves, and so forth—to keep your hands free. Depending on the durability of the belt material, you can use it for lashing, for climbing, for securing a splint, for the cord in a bow-and-drill fire kit, and many other possible uses.

Another is the belt knife. There are two basic types of belt knives. One is typified by the belt knife made by the Bowen company. The belt is heavy-duty leather, and the buckle itself is the handle of the small knife. The blade fits into a double layer of leather, so it is perfectly safe to wear. These are available in single or double edge, with the single edge being the most practical. Another style of belt knife consists of a knife that folds

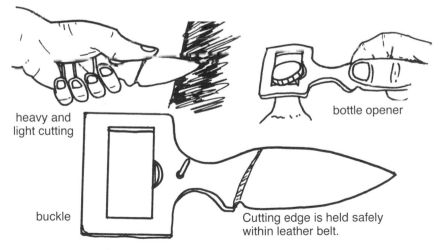

heavy and light cutting

bottle opener

buckle

Cutting edge is held safely within leather belt.

Bowen belt knife.

out of the buckle, leaving your belt still intact. In the Bowen-style, your belt is open when you use the knife, a fact that may or may not make a difference.

NOTE: *Some of these "belt knives" are illegal in some states. Check your local laws.*

I am partial to a belt made by an Amish leathersmith, Eli Miller, from Middlefield, Ohio. He also makes horse harnesses, and his people belts are as rugged and durable as a horse harness. If you are ever in rural Middlefield, Ohio, look him up out at Kinsman Road. You can also look in the Lehman's catalog (P.O. Box 41, Kidron, OH 44636) for some great belts. Many of the products in Lehman's catalog cater to the Amish and their penchant for self-reliance.

TIES

Ties are a carryover from the days when men wore ascots or kerchiefs, which were at least functional in their day. But the tie itself—a decorative piece of fabric that men wear around their necks to offset the boredom of their suits—hardly seems to have any survival value. In a survival situation, however, it *could* be used where a length of fabric is required, such as the cord in a bow-and-drill fire kit.

Ties do have the potential to be hazardous to our well-being. Consider that you are taking a nylon cord and tying it in a knot around your neck, and then tightening that knot. Keep those ties a bit on the loose side, and seriously consider wearing a snap-on tie. Every law enforcement agent who must wear a tie always wears a clip-on. Why? A tie is a handle with which your opponent can grab you and choke you. If there is a fight and someone grabs your snap-off tie, it pops right off.

KERCHIEF

Mention of the kerchief reminds us of cowboys. A kerchief is a unique multipurpose survival tool that is much more than decoration. If not worn around the neck, one should be carried at all times in the pocket, purse, briefcase, or pack.

When worn, it can prevent neckburn in the rear; when pulled over the nose, it protects from dust, smog, smoke, or blowing sand. It can also be worn as a headband or as a hat (especially for bald guys). I've seen

Kerchiefs for headband and neckerchief. DOUG HAIPT

Using a kerchief to filter dust or smoke. DOUG HAIPT

women at swimming holes who used two kerchiefs as a makeshift bathing top.

The kerchief is a napkin, a pot holder, a coffee filter, a water filter, a signaling flag, a gauze to stop bleeding, a makeshift "cord," and the list goes on and on.

Don't leave home without it!

HATS

Clearly, a good hat is a survival tool. It is not mere coincidence that so many people have worn so many types of hats.

Baseball hats are ubiquitous, and often can be had for free since everyone puts their advertising slogans on these hats. They are good for providing shade from the sun, which is important, but they don't do much else.

Probably the best style of hat is the cowboy-style hat with a large brim. Generally, you want a winter hat to be waterproof and to provide some insulation. You want a summer hat primarily to provide lots of shade.

SHELTER CONSIDERATIONS

THE BOTTOM LINE

- Shelters abound!
- Don't wait til it's dark before you start attempting to figure out your shelter for the night.
- Natural or man-made shelters that are ready-to-occupy are everywhere, and they should be your first choice. Why waste your energy if you do not need to?
- If there is nothing ready-to-occupy in the wilderness or city, start with the simplest shelter, a lean-to or a body hollow.

OK, hopefully, you'll grasp the fact that you should never leave home without dressing appropriately for survival. Your clothing is your shelter at a short distance.

But now, your house or apartment is destroyed, or you're lost in the woods. You're crying out loud, "Gimme shelter!"

URBAN SHELTERS

In the aftermath of an urban catastrophe, the type of shelter needed will depend on circumstances, location, and time of year.

After California's Northridge earthquake in 1994, many people in areas (both damaged and undamaged) were seen sleeping in their yards in backpacking tents. Once only the realm of backpacking shops, lightweight and inexpensive camping tents are now rather common. Granted, the really inexpensive tents aren't going to hold up for long periods of time from exposure to the sun, and they shouldn't be treated roughly. But they are good insurance against certain urban disasters, since they provide a simple shelter that can be installed in minutes.

Suggestion: Buy one slightly bigger than your expected needs—after a disaster, it is not uncommon to have unexpected guests. Also, take the time to set it up a few times so you know how to do it. Set it up in the dark also. Also consider getting a few inexpensive tube tents. They are lightweight and can easily be packed.

Also consider having a watertight box in your garage or back shed in which you store a few sleeping bags or blankets. The sleeping bags need not be ultralight and ultracompact. These are for backyard use in the event that your house in not safe to occupy.

Suppose you didn't take the time to purchase a tent and some sleeping bags? Then what? Again, this is one of those things that all depends on your location, time of year, and whether you are protecting yourself from the sun, the cold, the rain, the wind, the snow, the bugs, and so forth.

Are there scattered building materials around which can be collected and made into a makeshift shelter? Plywood, sheets of drywall, roofing tile, tarps, sheets of plastic, and so forth. I have seen some very ingenious homeless shelters throughout Los Angeles County that were watertight and made entirely of discards that had been collected on the streets. In some cases, the homeless person had a few tools with which to hold the shack together; in other cases, he or she used baling cord (the type of nylon cord used to tie bales of hay) to tie the whole thing together.

In the 1960s, I saw the incredible shack village on the edge of Tijuana, Mexico, where each "house" was a composite of tarps, galvanized sheet metal, corrugated metal and plastic, sheet plastic, plywood, and an amazing array of anything that could possibly be used to create a shelter. I know not if such structures still exist in Tijuana, but people throughout the world still live their lives in structures much less substantial than those shacks of Tijuana.

If you are uncertain about the types of quick emergency shelters that can be thrown up in a hurry, you can look at images of the multitude of shelters created throughout North America by the native Americans: wickiups, log cabins, tipis, hogans, cattail-covered shelters framed in willow, and many others.

Yes, our survival in the future can be based upon the wisdom of the past.

WILDERNESS SHELTERS

Depending on the size of your backyard, it is very possible that the type of shelter you might construct in the wilderness is exactly what you might build in the backyard. The type of shelter you make depends upon the number of people to be sheltered, the desired purpose of the shelter (will it be for working or just sleeping), the element(s) you want to be sheltered from (wind, rain, snow, cold, heat, sun, mosquitoes), and the availability of materials. This last one may be the strongest influence in what sort of shelter you actually build. After all, you can't build an igloo if you don't have any snow, and you can't build a small log cabin if you don't have a ready supply of suitable logs—to say nothing of an ax, experience, and so on.

But before we get too far along here, let's stop a second and take a look at our situation in the woods.

If we are contemplating building a shelter, this means we have already exhausted the possibility of going home tonight. Either we have determined that we are hopelessly lost, or the severe weather makes travel impossible.

Now, if you *haven't* carefully exhausted the option of getting back home—and getting back home is your desire—then you should definitely do whatever you can to get back home. Are there any landmarks that might help you get unlost? Is there a high peak you can climb in an attempt to determine where you are? If you're lost, we assume you don't have a map of the area and a compass. Have you tried making a simple sun compass in order to determine directions? (See page 245.) Are there any roads or highways nearby? Have you tried signaling with a mirror or making a smoky (but safe) fire?

These are just a very few of the things you can do in order to find your way home.

But—you have exhausted that possibility.

Before you go to all the trouble of building a wilderness shelter, you should first see if there are any ready-to-occupy shelters anywhere nearby. When you weren't lost, you probably were not looking at your terrain this way, but you need to reconsider if there was anything you saw that might be a good shelter for tonight.

There are plenty of natural and man-made shelter possibilities that you can find in the wilderness. Let's look at the man-made ones first.

MAN-MADE SHELTERS

How about an old abandoned car? Typically, the windows are all shattered when you find these in the wilderness. You have to clean the seats, and maybe encourage a few mice to spend the night elsewhere. These are not glamorous, but might keep you dry.

Abandoned cabins, utility shacks, and outbuildings abound in the wilderness. Even if locked, there may be a porch big enough to provide some shelter.

I know some of you will snicker at this, but I have spent a night in a remote outhouse. OK, it wasn't just a one seater. It was large enough that I could clean an area where I could comfortably sleep. The odor was not terribly bad, and I stayed dry as it rained outside.

Sleeping under bridges is also a possibility. I have done this while hitch-hiking. I have also spent nights in culverts and found them cozy and comfortable. These were not culverts in active use, however, but were the large cement tubes that had been stored near a road waiting to be installed. In another case, I slept in a culvert that was part of a child's playground. Active culverts are bad news, especially if it rains. You might get wet, washed away, or even killed.

There is often space under water towers where you can get out of the rain. There are a variety of water tower designs; some are better suited to survival camping than others.

NATURAL SHELTERS

Remember, depending on the circumstances, a shelter's requirements may vary. A rain shelter's requirements are different than a simple sun shelter. Still, naturally occurring shelters abound.

I have spent many nights in the inner recesses of large rock piles, in places such as Joshua Tree National Monument in California. These aren't caves in the normal sense of the word, but just places you can get into in order to get out of the incessant desert wind. It is slightly warmer in these spaces as well. Some of these will shelter you from rain, some will not. You can find such shelters widely throughout North America.

Phillip Thompson relaxes in the shade under the roots of a large alder.

Caves are generally a good choice, if it's really a cave and not a mine. Mines have very poor oxygen flow, and some have sudden drops where you might disappear. Mines can cave in more readily as well, since they are not natural, but simply tunnels that have been dug out of the hills. A cave in solid rock, where there is no dripping water, is usually a good shelter. Since these make good homes for all sorts of wildlife, look carefully for tracks and other signs to make sure the cave is not already occupied by larger creatures that may not like your presence. Caves—some very large—are found widely throughout North America.

Large hollow trees make great shelters. I spent a night in one during a heavy rainstorm and remained dry. Have you ever read *My Side of the Mountain* by Jean Craighead George? The young boy, Sam, goes to up-state New York and lives in a large hollow of a tree for a year. (It's a great tale of survival—highly recommended for children and adults.)

Even large fallen trees can be suitable shelters. Sometimes you can actually get into the hollow of the tree, or there may be enough space on one side and under to provide some quick shelter. One problem with fallen trees in the rain is that the rain flows around and under it, meaning, you'll still get wet under a large fallen tree.

An immediate shelter can be had under a thick pile of leaves or pine needles, especially in a dense forest. Such a shelter is good for protection against the cold.

MAKING YOUR OWN SHELTER

OK, you've concluded that there are no man-made and no natural shelters anywhere in your area. Or maybe it is so dark that you couldn't find them anyway. You've decided to build a shelter.

Though there are many possibilities, here are some very basic ideas. What you actually build depends on the availability of building materials, your mental and physical resources, and how much time you have to get a functional shelter constructed. For example, if it is starting to rain *now,* you simply need to act rapidly to produce some sort of shelter. Even if you don't think you'll spend the night in the woods in a rainstorm, you still may want some shelter. Being wet in the cold can lead to frostbite, hypothermia, and death.

Lean-Tos

The lean-to is a very basic shelter with many variations. It is so basic that even Bigfoot makes one, as I recall from the stories told around the campfire.

The easiest lean-to is begun by leaning a strong pole into the crotch of a tree. Then lean other poles onto each side. Continue to add poles, then brush, then leaves until you have a thick layer of insulation.

There's really nothing complicated about building a lean-to. The requirements are a good location (e.g., away from the water, naturally protected, an abundance of materials to use for building), the willingness to put in several hours of labor required to make a decent shelter, and a lack of concern about "getting dirty."

Once you've chosen the best location for your given area, begin by making the frame for the lean-to. This is either the pole leaned into the crotch of a tree, or leaned onto a stump, or even three poles tied together. Keep your ceiling low, especially if your primary purpose is to stay warm. All that extra ceiling space means a bigger shelter, which means it will take a lot longer to build, and will be a lot harder to get warm and stay warm.

The framework of a simple lean-to. JOE A. HALL

A simple lean-to.

A sweat lodge frame made from willow poles. Many Native American homes in the old days were begun with such a framework.

If there is rain, you'll want steeper walls to shed the rain. Layers of bark or corrugated material will help to shed the rain.

Body Hollows

Body hollows are another simple choice for a shelter when there are not a lot of trees and other brush to use. It does require a shovel or some digging instrument.

Dig a hole about the size of a grave, assuming one person. Make it larger if two or more will be occupying it. Line the bottom with lots of grass and other available insulation.

I have slept in these many times with open tops in the high desert. On the surface in the desert, it's colder and the wind blows constantly. Sand blows in your face. If you can dig a sleeping hole just a few feet below the

Jarrod Garrison
digs the hole for
a body hollow.
DUDE McLEAN

*Covering the hole
with branches.*
DUDE McLEAN

*Covering the
branches with
layers of leaves.*
DUDE McLEAN

Jarrod Garrison emerges from the nearly finished body hollow.
DUDE McLEAN

surface, it will be just a bit warmer and you won't have the sand blowing in your face all night. Even without a cover.

But if you have the option, you should build a cover over your body hollow. Begin by laying poles over the top of the shelter, leaving a space for your entrance. Once you have a "roof" of solid poles, you can begin adding brush, leaves, and successively smaller material.

Remember, the primitive shelters described here are not living shelters. They are what we might call glorified sleeping bags. They are a way to spend the night outside without freezing to death. You don't build such a shelter with a lot of air space. You build them tight and compact. You make such a shelter only as large as needed and no bigger.

Snow Cave

A snow cave is simply a burrow dug into a drift of snow. Though you *could* just dig a hole in the snow and sleep in it, it is not ideal. A big hole in the snow could perhaps be covered and that would improve its efficiency. But remember that cold sinks while heat rises. A hole in the snow is a refrigerator, and it's not the best snow shelter.

Look for thick snow on a hillside or in a valley. Burrow a horizontal tunnel in a few feet—and then begin to dig out the ceiling. Continue to dig out the snow until you have a comfortable hollow in the snow. You want the entry to the cave to be at the lowest part of the cavity. This allows your heat to be trapped within the snow cave and it will be a warmer experience.

I have dug a snow cave suitable for spending the night in a little over an hour. You don't sleep directly on the snow since you will lose body heat that way. You must place a tarp on the floor of the snow cave, or use a thick layer of whatever leaves are available. Pine needles are typically

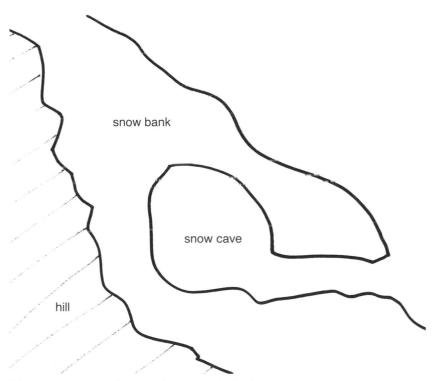

snow bank

snow cave

hill

The snow cave is a burrow dug into a drift of snow.

BUILDING AN AUTHENTIC IGLOO
The ultimate winter survival shelter

The igloo is the best shelter in winter snow conditions. It's strong, wind-resistant, and can be kept warm. When more snow falls on it, the igloo gets even stronger.

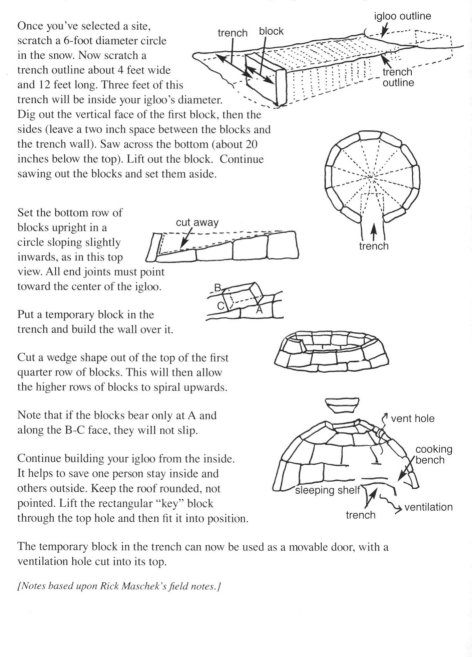

Once you've selected a site, scratch a 6-foot diameter circle in the snow. Now scratch a trench outline about 4 feet wide and 12 feet long. Three feet of this trench will be inside your igloo's diameter. Dig out the vertical face of the first block, then the sides (leave a two inch space between the blocks and the trench wall). Saw across the bottom (about 20 inches below the top). Lift out the block. Continue sawing out the blocks and set them aside.

Set the bottom row of blocks upright in a circle sloping slightly inwards, as in this top view. All end joints must point toward the center of the igloo.

Put a temporary block in the trench and build the wall over it.

Cut a wedge shape out of the top of the first quarter row of blocks. This will then allow the higher rows of blocks to spiral upwards.

Note that if the blocks bear only at A and along the B-C face, they will not slip.

Continue building your igloo from the inside. It helps to save one person stay inside and others outside. Keep the roof rounded, not pointed. Lift the rectangular "key" block through the top hole and then fit it into position.

The temporary block in the trench can now be used as a movable door, with a ventilation hole cut into its top.

[Notes based upon Rick Maschek's field notes.]

available at the higher elevations where you might need a snow cave, and they can be matted down on the floor.

A snow cave is really that simple! Is there a danger of suffocation or of a collapse? Suffocation is highly unlikely. You should be able to stay in the cave for a few days without any need to punch any air holes. A collapse is possible if there is a landslide and you are in its path. Otherwise, if you built your snow cave with rather thin walls, it might collapse inward as the inside of the cave warmed up. Whether such a collapse is life-threatening depends upon what is happening outside the cave. If suddenly you are exposed to high winds and very low temperatures, you may have to rapidly put plan B into action.

An Igloo

Unlike a snow cave, the igloo has structural integrity, and you could stand on top of it without it collapsing. I learned how to make an igloo from Rick Maschek, who was a search and rescue team member of the high desert.

Rick taught us that you first select an ideal location for the igloo. You draw a circle in the snow that will accommodate however many people

Building an igloo.

A nearly finished igloo.

Except for the arch over the entrance, this igloo is done. It took seven people two hours to build (no one in this group had ever made an igloo before).

need shelter. You then begin to cut rectangular blocks of snow, and place them so their long end is on the circle you drew. These are actually trapezoidal, not rectangular, with the sides tapered slightly inward so each block fits together snuggly when made into a circle.

Once you have one row of snow blocks, you remove one half of one block with a diagonal cut from a top corner to a lower corner. You then continue adding blocks by putting the next block into this diagonal spot, and then the blocks spiral upward. You must lean each block more and more inward as you spiral upward, despite the fact that you will not think the snow can stick to itself so well.

A few clues: One person goes inside to receive each block, and make sure the edges where they meet are cut clean so they fit snug. It is also important to keep the top leading edge of the igloo flat as you go, otherwise you will be unable to continue spiraling with the blocks.

Refer to the pictures here and try it sometime on your own. If you think you will ever need a functional igloo, do not wait until the emergency is upon you. Gather your friends and family together and go out and make sport of this learning process.

5

The World Is Tied Together with Fiber

Captain Kirk (upon landing on an unknown planet):
"Spock, check to see if we can use those vines for
bow strings."
Spock: "These vines have suitable tensile cohesion."
Kirk: "But can we use them for bow strings?"
Spock: "I believe I just answered that."

THE VALUE OF FIBER IN PRIMITIVE CULTURES
AND SURVIVAL SITUATION

It has been said that the world of the ancient ones was tied together with fiber. This statement was true both literally and figuratively.

Though it is literally true, it is a point lost on modern city folks who only think of some dietary concept whenever you mention "fiber." In the modern world, the ability to extract fiber from raw nature is fast becoming a lost art since virtually everything we use is made by someone else, far away. Our clothes are made in factories. We never see the cotton on the farm, the wool, or the various other fibers made into sheets of fabric. And modern fastening devices—Velcro, buttons, zippers—have given us even less reason to consider the everyday value of ties.

Such was not always the case.

In preindustrialized societies, one's very clothing would be made from weaving various plant fibers together into skirts or robes or more complicated garments. Various types of sandals have been woven for millennia from local leaves, roots, or bark.

Fiber was also used in home construction, whether a simple dome-shaped grass covered house, or a templelike house built from bamboo with the bamboo secured with stout vines.

Fibers were woven into all manner of carrying bags, packs, sacks, fishing nets, snares, traps, and cordage for the bow strings. Fiber was everywhere in nature, and each was chosen for each application based on the suitability determined by everyday experience.

It is a sad fact that we have so lost this basic knowledge that not one in a hundred campers carries along cordage or rope anymore. I have long considered that the "holy trinity" of must carry items includes a knife (primitive or modern), a fire starter (primitive or modern), and twine of some type. I also consider the ability to find or make all three of these from the wilderness to be the first skills that anyone should master.

Fibers make life easier, such as mats for sleeping or even sleeping bags. I once made a primitive loom in my parents' backyard and wove together two large rectangular cattail mats. I then wove the two mats together on three sides and slept that night in my somewhat cool cattail sleeping bag.

Basketry has become an art and science in its own right. Depending on your skill level, you can create a simple container in a few minutes or a beautiful work of art that would be the equivalent of money in primitive societies. Depending on your intended use, the materials for each basket, as well as the design, are specifically selected.

These are some of the literal ways in which fibers were everywhere in the life of ancient peoples.

But fiber played another role. Keep in mind, that we are speaking of at least three discrete (though related) skills. First is the ability to identify these plants. Next is the ability to process the fibers. Last is the ability to actually weave and manufacture the intended product. In general, I have only been speaking of the third skill so far.

In the past when "work" was done, people sat for hours and hours preparing fibers for later use. While washing or working the various leaves, twining very long cords, or doing the basketry, sandal weaving, or bow string making, the elders of the clan passed on their wisdom and philosophy to the young. This might take the form of oral traditions. But an even easier way to pass on traditions is through the specificity of certain crafts, such as weaving and basketry. Symbols can be incorporated into woven objects that serve as a mnemonic device for each generation to pass along as a living tradition to the next. Sometimes legominisms are woven into fabrics, cloth, baskets, or other art objects. These are symbols that are clear enough for anyone to see, but whose meaning requires some training to interpret. These are just a few of the ways in which the life of our ancestors was tied together with fiber.

PROCESSING FIBER FROM PLANT MATERIALS

CATTAILS (WHOLE LEAVES)
Cattails are easy to work with and they grow everywhere. They do not have high tensile strength, so their use is limited to baskets, sandals, mats, but usually not rope that would be under pressure.

Cut them while they are green, and let them dry for a few days. They will change from green to a dull green or tan color, and they will shrink a little. Moisten them, and then begin your weaving.

NETTLES (AND OTHER INNER BARK FIBER FROM STALKS)
Nettles are also common, but you need to carefully handle them so you don't get stung. Collect the tall stalks—they can be used fresh or dried. Wet the stalks and gently pound them with a rounded wooden club or mallet. This releases just the fiber, which you can now twine, braid, or weave into an end product.

YUCCA (AND OTHER LEAF FIBERS)
Yucca leaves can be used green or dried; it somewhat depends on your need and the end product.

To use green leaves, cut off the individual leaf and shred it between the hands. Then agitate it in water and rub the leaf back and forth between your hands to leave just the fiber. Then make rope, sandals, or other products, remembering that the fiber will shrink somewhat.

The dead leaves are also abundant. Collect them and then rub each leaf over a smooth branch or a metal pole. This will cause lots of dust and you'll be left with good fiber. Once processed this way, you can wet it (for pliability) and then weave baskets, rope, and the like.

MAKING PRODUCTS FROM PLANT FIBERS

TWINE

Making twine is a good first project, since that twine can then be used in most other projects. Even the twine itself may be needed for any of a hundred or so uses.

To begin, you can tie off one bundle of fibers, or you can simply bend a bundle in the middle. You need to have two equal sections. Then, twist the right half (we'll call it A) to the right, and pull it to the left over the top of the other fiber section (called B). Now the untwisted section (B) is on the right. So twist B to the right and again pull it to the left over the top of A. Simply repeat this over and over, twisting the segment on the right to the right, and pulling it to the left over the top. This is twining.

You can make this any thickness you need, and you can make this as long as needed by adding new fibers periodically.

The middle of a thin bundle of yucca fibers are held by the nail. The right side is being twisted to the right. AMY WOODRUFF

The right strand has now been pulled to the left, over the other strand. The strand that had been on the left is now on the right.
AMY WOODRUFF

The process continues. The right strand is twisted to the right, and then pulled to the left over the other strand. AMY WOODRUFF

Just keep saying, "Twist to the right, pull to the left." You are only working the right side, twisting it to the right, pulling it to the left, over and over and over.
AMY WOODRUFF

The process continues.
AMY WOODRUFF

New strands are added. When you are nearing the end of your fibers, you add a new strand by simply laying it into the opening of the two existing strands, and continuing to "twist to the right, pull to the left."
AMY WOODRUFF

Glendale Community College hiking class students learn to make twine from yucca.
TIMOTHY SNIDER

The author (right) shows student how to make yucca twine. DOUG HAIPT

BRAID

Women have it over men on this one, since the majority of women not only know how to braid, but they could do it in the dark! (Think about that.) It matters not what sort of fiber you are using to braid, whether it is plant fibers, hair, or rags.

Though there are many types of braids, we'll review the simple three-ply braid.

Collect a bundle of fibers and tie them off at one end. It helps if someone can hold the end or if you secure the bundle to a post or something secure. Divide the fiber into three equal sections. Hold the bundle so that three sections flow downward from the top. You have a strand on the right, in the middle, and on the left. Now, take the strand on the right and place it between the other two strands. Then take the strand on the left and put it

Braiding begins with three strands. You could use strands of bed sheets, leather, plastic, bark, and so on. In this case, thin yucca leaves are used. The yucca strand on the right is about to be moved. AMY WOODRUFF

The strand on the right has now been moved into the middle of the other two. AMY WOODRUFF

Now the left strand has been moved in to the middle of the other two strands. AMY WOODRUFF

Now the right strand has been moved into the middle of the other two strands. AMY WOODRUFF

The process continues. You take the strand from the right side and put it between the other two. Then you take the strand from the left side and you put it between the other two. AMY WOODRUFF

Repeat this a hundred times or so and then you have a braid!
AMY WOODRUFF

We're about ⅓ of the way to a belt!
AMY WOODRUFF

between the other two strands. Then take the right strand and place it between the other two strands, and continue on in the same manner. That's braiding.

SANDALS

There are many possible fiber sandal designs that have been employed over the world, depending on the available supplies. Where palms are available, simple over and under weave sandals have been used.

One of the designs used in the West and Southwest of the United States is the thick yucca sandals. Begin with the processed fiber. Starting with a thick cord, bend it into a "U" shape, slightly bigger than the foot, with the open end being the heel. Then secure another cord to the toe area and weave this back and forth, over and under the two sides of the sandal, until you achieve the desired shape. After the heel of the sandal is finished, add straps to secure the sandal to the ankle and over the top of the foot. Typically, these attachments did not go through the toe, but that method is sometimes used in modern reproductions.

Student at a weaving workshop makes a yucca sandal in the chumash style.

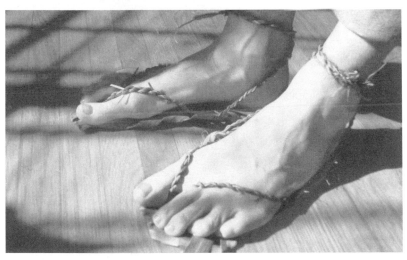

Mogollon-style yucca sandals. KARYL NEWMAN

BASKETS—COILED

Remember: a weave is a weave—it can be done with natural fibers, with paper, with rags, with anything that works. Once you know the weaves, you can make the objects and try countless variations of those objects.

Making coiled baskets is a specific procedure, nowadays often using pine needles. This procedure was widespread traditionally and is suitable for lots of other fibers. Also, you can use that basic weave to make footwear, packs, plates, and so on.

There are some excellent books available devoted exclusively to this topic. One is *Pine Needle Basketry: From Forest Floor to Finished Project* by Judy Mofield Mallow.

But, in a nutshell, here is the procedure. Collect good pine needles, then wash and dry them. Begin by creating a small, round button shape from one

Allison starts on a coiled pine needle basket.

end of the needles by wrapping them with raffia, cattail, yucca, or whatever you are using. Continue to coil the needles, and wrap the needles with the raffia, wrapping so that each new coil is sewn into the previous coil.

After you have made a few of these, you try to improve the tightness of the weave, the symmetry of the wrapping, and the evenness of the continuous thickness of pine needles.

For my very first coil basket, I went to the Southwest Museum and purchased a little kit with a needle, raffia, pine needles, and an instruction booklet for making one specific sort of basket. After you follow the instructions and see how easy it was, you begin to wonder why you wasted your money on the silly kit, but you won't come to that realization until you've done the work and earned that insight. After that, you'll just go find the abundant pine needles available for the collecting.

The author shows a pine needle coiled basket in progress.
DUDE McLEAN

*Master weaver
Lois Rainwater
shows two of her
favorite coiled
baskets.*

BASKETS—WOVEN

There are many, many styles of traditional basketry that employ many different weaves such as twining, randing, wicker, and so on. The basic "over and under" weave is just one of many. Again, there are some excellent sources out there. Two good books are *Pomo Basketmaking: A Supreme Art for the Weaver* by Elsie Allen (Happy Camp, CA: Naturegraph Publishers, 1972) and *Indian Basketry* by George Wharton James (Kessinger Publishing).

Probably the best way to get started on basket making is to enroll in a local class where you will be able to actually create one while the teacher

The author shows how to start a basket with cattails. DOUG HAIPT

The author works on an "over-and-under" basket, in yucca. DOLORES LYNN NYERGES

A simple basket made with periwinkle vines.
DUDE McLEAN

The Angle family shows the baskets they made from periwinkle vine. Geoff Angle (left) also displays a yucca sandal.
DUDE McLEAN

watches and corrects you. It will be an all-day class or longer, but that's what it takes.

MATS

There are many ways to create a simple floor mat. Anyone who can remember "over and under and over and under" should be able to figure it out, given enough time.

Still, there are some techniques that make it go easier. Mats can be made on the loom described below or they can be done all by hand. Start with a post or two-by-four to which you can secure as many cords or strings as needed. I often use cattail leaves. If you place them very close, you will have a tight weave. If they are spread out, you will have a mat that is quicker to make but with a looser weave. It all depends on your needs.

Once all the cords are tied to the post, then secure that post to something so it doesn't move around. Stake it to the ground or secure it to a tree. Then begin on one end and weave cattail or whatever over and under and over and under. When you get to the end, come back the opposite way, being sure that you are alternating your over and under from the previous line.

Once you get the hang of it, it is a somewhat rote, monotonous activity. It takes time.

When your goal is simply a mat, you can use almost any fiber. High tensile strength is not required.

A Simple Loom

Emphasis is on the word "simple" here. There are some complex looms—such as the Navajo rug looms—that take several hours just to set up. If you want to learn how to do that, I strongly suggest you enroll in a college class where you get lots of hands-on experience. Don't try to just read about it in a book—you'll be more confused with a book than before you started!

But there is a simple loom that can be made with twine and sticks. A picture is worth a thousand words, as they say, but here are the details.

Assume you want to make a simple mat, say four feet by eight feet, give or take. You'll be making the mat from cattails. First, tie a pole, slightly longer than four feet, onto a tree, about a foot or so off the ground and horizontal to the ground. Secure it well. Next, tie ten cords onto this pole. Each cord should be at least ten feet long. (You could have six cords, you could have twenty cords—this is just an example.) Tie the cords onto the horizontal pole, and space them evenly. Now tie all these cords onto another horizontal pole (an old broom handle works well), again evenly spaced. When all ten cords are tied, the tension on each string should be pretty much the same.

Next, pull the free horizontal pole so the cords are stretched out, and lay it on the ground. Now drive stakes into the ground between each of the cords. That means nine stakes in this case. These stakes should rise above the ground about two feet. Now, tie one cord from the top of each stake to the corresponding point on the pole that you secured to the tree.

Okay, now, when done, you will have nine secure cords lashed to stakes in the ground, connected to the pole on the tree. You will also have another ten cords, also connected to the pole on the tree and tied to a movable pole.

Now, note that you can lift the free pole up and down. Place cattails into the "V" of the cords, up against the tree, and then drop the free pole so the cattails are wrapped. Then put more cattails into the "V" again and continue until you reach the length you desire. When done, tie off the cords and cut it free. The loom became a part of the mat. This is simple and can be set up in an hour. You can make quickie mats this way, or you can make finer fabrics. It all depends on what materials you have to work with and what you are trying to achieve.

SHELTERS

Fibers of plants have also been used in the manufacture of many traditional houses and shelters. In Southern California, the Native Americans built dome-shaped structures from poles, such as willow. Then bundles of cattail fiber were lashed to the poles from the bottom up, to create a shingled effect and produce a waterproof shelter. Native Americans living where palms grew, such as in the Southwest deserts, used the palm leaves to create a thatched roof.

These are just a few ways in which fibers are used to "tie one's home together."

*Amman show the
net bag he wove, in
which he's
carrying his
periwinkle basket.*
DUDE McLEAN

CONCLUSIONS

The world is tied together with fiber—at least so it was once upon a time when we lived our lives with less material comfort, where form followed function, where meaning and allegory were sought and found in the sheer pragmatism of everyday objects. Though we have not completely lost this function of the ordinary, this way of thinking and doing is fast disappearing as the world becomes more and more materialistic as its only function.

That things are never what they seem to be is true with fiber. Delve into the fibers and explore their nuances of use, function, and meaning. They are your link to the wisdom of the past and to the collective wisdom that is timeless. Learning the nearly lost arts of using fibers is not "living in the past." Past is prologue to future.

COMPARISON OF COMMON FIBER PLANTS

	Part used	How to process	Tensile strength*	Length of fibers
Agaves *Agave* spp. **False Agave** *Furcraea* spp.	Leaf	Bake, then shred leaf, and wash out fiber	93	Very long, up to three feet
Barks, various Numerous spp.	Bark, usually the inner bark	Depends on type of bark; generally, pull off, twist	45 to 70	Varies
Cattail *Typha latifolia;* Related *Typha* spp.	Leaf	Dry, moisten, then use	45	Up to six feet
Dogbane (Indian Hemp) *Apocynum* spp.	Inner bark	Gently pound stems	80	Up to one foot
Grasses Numerous spp.	Leaf and stem	When dried, moisten, then use	45 to 80	Varies
Milkweed *Asclepia Syriaca*	Stem	Gently pound stems	70	Several inches to one foot
Nettle *Urtica* spp.	Stem	Gently pound stems	65	Several inches to one foot
Palms Numerous spp.	Leaf	Generally, moisten the dried leaves before use	45	Varies
Pine Needles *Pinus* spp.	Needles	Collect, clean, allow to dry, moisten before using	40	Up to a one-foot maximum
Roots, Various Numerous spp.	Roots	Varies	45 to 80	Varies

*Tensile strength figures are based on general experience and specific testing. Strength is determined by how much pressure is required to break a fiber that is ¼ inch thick. Scale is 1 to 100, with 1 being the weakest and 100 virtually unbreakable. Keep in mind that no two plants of the same species will respond exactly the same to testing. We would appreciate commentary from readers about these relative tensile strengths. For some applications, tensile strength is not important (e.g., mats).

How best used	Where found	Cautions and comments
Cordage, sandals, heavy-duty uses	Southwest and elsewhere as ornamentals	Juice from fresh agave leaf causes serious rashes in many people
Used as is for lashing, woven into cordage, in some cases made directly into containers (e.g., birch)	Worldwide	Since barks are everywhere, this is worthy of experimentation
Mats, shelter coverings, non-stress applications	Worldwide in wet areas	Good for applications not under stress
Cordage, bow strings	Rare, but widespread across United States	Good bow string material: *"A premier native plant fibre"* (Tamara Wilder)
All cordage applications	Worldwide	
Cordage	Throughout the United States	The sap causes irritation to some people
Cordage, fiber	Worldwide	Be careful of the formic acid when gathering
Basketry, mats	Southwest; widespread as ornamental	
Baskets	Worldwide	Primarily baskets and non-stress applications
Baskets, cordage	Worldwide	Worth experimenting

This list is by no means complete. Many localized native, cultivated, or ornamental fiber plants, for example, have not been included. Barks, roots, and vines are generic categories. Comments made are general since there are diverse qualities of fibers depending on the individual plant source.

COMPARISON OF COMMON FIBER PLANTS continued

	Part used	How to process	Tensile strength	Length of fibers
Rush/Bulrush *Scirpus validus; S. acutus*	Stems	Dry, split, then moisten before use	55	Up to eight feet
Seaweeds All members of red, brown, and green marine algae	Stipes ("stems")	Varies; typically, dry and then oil before use	40 to 75	Varies; some are quite long
Vines, Various Numerous spp.	Stems	Typically these are "ready to go"	35 to 85	Varies; we have collected vines fifty feet long
Willow *Salix* spp.	Stems	Dry, split, moisten	85	Stems can be many feet long
Yucca *Yucca* spp.	Leaves	Shred leaves, moisten, then weave or twine	95	About three feet

Special thanks to Tamara Wilder who read a draft of this chart and made suggestions and corrections.

How best used	Where found	Cautions and comments
Mats, baskets, boats, house coverings	Mostly along waterways, oceans	Good for nonstress uses; hollow stems will float
Nets, sandals, cordage	All coastal areas	Not all seaweeds can be used this way; must experiment
Lashing, cordage, bow strings, baskets, etc.	Various ones found worldwide	Be sure you can recognize the poisonous vines (e.g., poison ivy, poison oak)
Baskets, part of crafts	Worldwide, typically near water	
Cordage, bow string, sandals, clothing	West and Southwestern United States	One of the best overall fiber sources

6

Food

Food is usually not the thing that makes the difference between life and death. At least not in short-term survival situations. The things we need most in a survival situation are those things typically hardest to obtain at the time: we need water in the desert, we need warmth in the snow, we need fire when it is raining, and so on.

Food is essential to life, of course, but we can get by on very little. If we have good water, we can get by even longer.

Still, our life revolves around food and drink. It is what we do around the campfire while sharing stories with our friends. It is what we do at Thanksgiving, Christmas, Hanukkah, birthdays, and all the holidays and Holy Days when family gathers. We infuse food with something special, and we share that something special when we gather to talk and dine.

So from a survival standpoint, though food is not high on the list of immediate needs, it is still a need to deal with. And food is everywhere. If we don't see it, we haven't been looking.

GETTING STARTED

EXPLORING THE FASCINATING WORLD OF WILD PLANTS

During the many field trips and classes that I have conducted, I have often been asked how I got interested in the subject of edible wild plants, and if I could provide some hints for learning about wild plants in the quickest and most accurate way possible.

Though I have spent long hours studying books and taking high school and college classes, my quick and primary source of learning has always

---

FOOD IN THE WILDERNESS

- *Animals.* Nearly all animals can be eaten: insects, larvae, fish, snakes, lizards, birds, rabbits, squirrels, and all larger game. There are countless ways to capture these animals. Always cook them.
- *Plants.* Don't eat any plants you don't know. Take the time to learn plants one at a time, and make the effort to learn the most important plant families. There are *no* 100 percent foolproof quickie rules of thumb for determining edibility. Don't even consider eating any wild mushrooms unless you've spent at least two years actively studying them.
- Remember, you can study plants every day by learning all the wild and domestic plants that grow where you live. Begin using them one by one, and try them in different ways.

---

been direct field experience with an expert. Thinking that I knew "a lot," I have been humbled many times to encounter flora that appeared totally unfamiliar to me in a field or on a mountainside only a few miles away. Gradually, little by little, I came to know the plants of the fields, the chaparral, the mountains, the ocean areas, the deserts.

In time, the more I researched the uses of plants, it was obvious that peoples in the past were concerned about much more than eating. *And plants played a key role in just about every skill or art in the old days.* Various plants provided materials for making fire, soap, fiber and weaving materials, shelter, for clothing, and medicine, as well as for stunning fish. My goal has always been to enhance my understanding of how people did things in the past in the context of enhancing the quality of my life today, in today's living circumstances.

Don't forget that when we are speaking of survival skills, *the knowledge of food plants is arguably the least important, while also being arguably one of the hardest to master.* It is the least important because we can get by for a long time without food, and anyone should know that you can eat just about any animal—but you can't randomly eat any plant. It is the hardest to master simply because there are so many plants from place to place. Lots of memorization is involved. So what's the best way for a beginner to make progress with plants?

First, don't worry about trying to know everything at once. The best way to get started is have a skilled naturalist or botanist go on a walk with you in your own backyard or neighborhood, somewhere close to where you live. Take lots of notes and photos. Regularly review those plants you saw in your neighborhood walk. Observe their changes throughout the seasons so you know what they look like as a sprout, as an adolescent, as a mature and flowering plant, in fruit, and when dead. This is the sort of awareness that you cannot get from a book. It can only be gained by experience.

And don't worry about all those seemingly exciting plants that you heard about from the rain forest or from China during some college seminar. Learn about what you see every day. Even twenty miles away is too far. Get to know the plants in your own backyard, in your own neighborhood. Get to know them like friends. Ask questions regularly of whomever is teaching you. Begin to use one plant at a time in your meals—one plant that you absolutely, unequivocally know is an edible wild plant.

You don't need to make entire meals from wild plants. Just begin by introducing one wild plant into your normal meals. You might use the plant in a salad, in a soup, in a vegetable dish, in a stew. Get to know it. Then, repeat this with another plant. Yes, at first, you'll just be learning to recognize ONE plant at a time until you get to know it intimately, till you can spot it while driving by in a car.

Believe it or not, most of what are called common weeds are edible, and are today found worldwide. Thus, some of the likely plants you'll be tasting in the beginning will be plants such as lamb's-quarter, sow thistle, purslane, curly dock, dandelion, chicory, cactus, acorns, watercress, cattails, onions, wild grasses, mustards, and more.

THERE ARE NO SHORTCUTS

It is to your advantage to completely disregard any of the rules of thumb you've ever been taught about plant identification—you know, the shortcuts for determining whether or not a plant is edible. The shortcuts are things like if a plant has a milky sap, it is not edible. If a plant causes an irritation in the mouth when you eat a little, it is not safe to eat. If the animals eat the plants or berries, they are safe to eat. If the berries are white they are poisonous; if the berries are black or blue, they are safe to eat. And on and on. Disregard all these shortcuts since—although often based on some fact—they all have exceptions. There are no shortcuts to what is necessary: You must study, and you will need field experience.

One of the more foolish shortcuts that I hear repeated over and over is that if you do not know the identity of a particular plant, you can try a sort of taste test to determine edibility. This is foolhardy for many reasons. A small amount of poison hemlock will kill you quickly. And a genuine survival situation is not the time to experiment with your body as your guinea pig. Why would you want to risk getting sick in a survival situation? Furthermore, for such a taste test to be meaningful, your stomach should be empty for about eight hours. That means if you have food that you *can* eat, you'd need to *not eat* that food in order for your "self-experiment" to be meaningful.

Look folks—get over it! There are no shortcuts. You *must* study, and you *must* put in your hours of field experience.

LEARN THE FAMILIES
If there is any sort of shortcut to the study of plants, it is to learn to recognize plant families, and learn to know which families are entirely safe for consumption. Beyond that, you must learn plants one by one for absolute safety.

I strongly suggest that you take at least a college course in botany (preferably, taxonomy) so you get to know how botanists designate plant families. This will enable you to look at my list of safe families, and then by using the books written by botanists of the flora of your area (there are such books for all parts of the country) check to see which plants in your area belong to any of the completely safe families. Eventually, you'll look at a plant and examine it and you'll know which family it likely belongs to.

Again, there is no magical key that will make all of this effortless. Learn plants one by one, then begin to learn the edible families, one by one. Get a botanical flora book written for your area and study it. Do your own field work, ideally with someone who already knows the plants.

Gradually you will be using more and more wild plants for food and medicine, and perhaps for soap, fiber, fire, and so on.

Some plant families are difficult to recognize unless you are a trained botanist, but there are some good learning tools out there. For example, I strongly recommend you get a copy of Tom Elpel's *Botany in a Day* and read it. I listed fourteen of the easiest to recognize families as an appendix to my *Guide to Wild Foods* book. My original research was done with the assistance of Dr. Leonid Enari, who was one of my teachers and the chief botanist at the L.A. County Arboretum in Arcadia, California, for many years.

A WORLDWIDE GUIDE TO NATURE'S FOODS

	Description	Parts used	Food uses
Acorns *Quercus* spp.	The fruit of the oak tree	Acorns (nuts)	1. Flour; 2. pickles; 3. mush
Cacti Cactacea (Cactus family)	Succulent desert plants of various shapes	1. Tender parts; 2. fruit	1. Salad; 2. cooked vegetable; 3. omelet; 4. desserts; drinks
Cattails *Typha* spp.	Reedlike plants; fruit looks like hotdog on a stick	1. Pollen; 2. green flower, spike; 3. tender shoots; 4. rhizome	1. Flour; 2. cooked vegetable; 3. salad; 4. flour
Chickweed *Stellaria media*	Weak-stemmed, opposite leaves, five-petaled flower	Entire tender plant	1. Salad; 2. tea
Dandelion *Taraxacum officinale*	Low plant, toothed leaves, conspicuous yellow flower	1. Roots; 2. leaves	1. Cooked vegetable; 2. coffeelike beverage; 3. salad; 4. cooked vegetable
Dock *Rumex crispus*	Long leaves with wavy margins	1. Leaves; 2. stems; 3. seeds	1. Salad; 2. cooked vegetable; 3. pie; 4. flour

The attached chart, A Worldwide Guide to Nature's Foods, was inspired by my friend Jay Watkins and based upon my research with Dr. Leonid Enari. Granted, there are many more than a dozen, but as Jay and I discussed this idea, I decided to focus on twelve plants that could be found not just anywhere in the United States, but in most locales throughout the entire world. This chart's function is not identification, per se, but to give you an overview of these common plants. Anyone who has studied wild foods for a few years is probably already familiar with these dozen easiest-to-recognize, most widespread, and most versatile wild foods.

Preparation	Benefits	Where found	When found
1. Leach out tannic acid first; 2. then grind	Similar to potatoes	Mountains, valleys	Fall
1. Carefully remove spines; 2. dice or slice as needed	Pads said to be good for diabetics; fruits rich in sugar	Dry desertlike environments; Mediterranean zones	Young greens in spring and summer; fruit in summer and fall
1. Shake out pollen; 2. boil; 3. remove outer green fibrous parts; 4. remove outer parts, crush	Widespread, versatile	Wet areas, e.g., roadside ditches, marshes	Spring through fall
1. Clip; 2. rinse; 3. add dressing or make infusion	Good diuretic	Common and widespread when moisture is present	Spring and summer
1. Clean and cook; or dry, roast, grind; 2. clean and make desired dish	Richest source of beta-carotene; very high in vitamin A	Common in lawns and fields	Best harvested in spring
1. Clean; 2. use like rhubarb; 3. winnow seeds	Richer in vitamin C than oranges	Common in fields and near water	Spring through fall

A WORLDWIDE GUIDE TO NATURE'S FOODS continued

	Description	Parts used	Food uses
Grasses Gramineae (Grass family)	Many widespread varieties	1. Seeds; 2. leaves	1. Flour 2. mush; 3. salad; 4. juiced; 5. cooked vegetable
Lamb's-quarter *Chenopodium album*	Triangular leaves with toothed margins, mealy surface	1. Leaves; 2. tender stems; 3. seeds	1. Salad; 2. soup; 3. omelets; 4. cooked; 5. bread; 6. mush
Mustard *Brassica* spp.; Cruciferae (mustard family)	Variable leaves with large terminal lobes; four-petaled flowers	1. Leaves; 2. seeds; 3. some roots	1. Salads; 2. cooked dishes; 3. as a seasoning
Onions *Allium* spp.	Grasslike appearance; flowers with three petals, three sepals	1. Leaves; 2. bulbs	1. Seasoning; 2. salad; 3. soup; 4. vegetable dishes
Purslane *Portulaca oleracea*	Low growing succulent, paddle-shaped leaves	All tender portions	1. Salad; 2. sautéed; 3. pickled; 4. soup; 5. vegetable dishes
Seaweeds Brown, red, and green marine algae (Phaeophyceae, Rhodophyceae, Chlorophyceae familes)	Marine algae of many shapes and colors	Entire plant	Depending on seaweed: 1. Salad; 2. soup; 3. stew; 4. broth

For more detailed descriptions of the above plants, see *In The Footsteps of Our Ancestors: Guide to Wild Foods* by Christopher Nyerges, or *Botany in a Day* by Tom Elpel.

You'll note that several of the entries represent not just an individual plant, but rather a plant family or a large group of plants.

Preparation	Benefits	Where found	When found
1. Harvest and winnow; 2. harvest, clean, chop	1. Easy to store; 2. rich in many nutrients	Common in all environments	Fall and spring
1. Harvest, clean; 2. winnow the seeds	Rich in vitamin A and calcium	Likes disturbed rich soils	Spring through fall
1. Gather, clean; 2. Look as needed	Said to help prevent cancer	Common in fields and many environments	Spring through fall
Clean, remove tough outer leaves	Good for reducing high blood pressure and high cholesterol level	Some varieties found in all environments	Spring is best
Rinse off any soil	Richest source of omega-3 fatty acids	Common in parks, gardens, disturbed soils	Summer
Use dried, raw, or cooked, depending on species	Excellent source of iodine; great salt substitute	Oceans	Year-round

This is the case with acorns, for there are several hundred species of oak trees. Cacti, grasses, and seaweeds are likewise large groups of plants, not individuals. Cattail is actually a family, called the Cattail Family, of which there are two species. With mustard, we could be referring to just the genus *Brassica,* which are the plants we normally call mustard, or we could be referring to the entire Mustard Family, none of which are toxic, and most of which are readily palatable. Onions are not a family, but a subgroup of the Lily Family.

This overview should help both beginners as well as specialists.

Acorns

Every child knows how to recognize acorns—the fruit of the oak tree. They are found worldwide. Collect the acorns in the fall. They are easiest to shell if they are dried a bit first, which can be done in the sun or in an oven. When dry, whack each one with a rock to remove the shell. The insides must then be leached, which means you need to get rid of the bitter tannic acid. There are many ways to do this, but here is how I do it.

I keep the shelled acorns whole and I either boil them for the better part of an hour until they are no longer bitter (changing the water every five to ten minutes) or I soak them in a big pot outside for about a month. When I simply soak, I change the water in the morning and at night. This may take up to a month before the acorns are no longer bitter.

An acorn. Before leaching, it must be shelled.

Tara grinds manzanita berries to be added to acorn flour.
MARIA REDINGER

Next, while the acorns are still wet, I run them through a meat grinder to produce a coarse meal. I dry this and store it in bottles. I grind it finer in a wheat grinder if I need flour, or I add it as-is to cookie or cake batter, or soup. In general, you can mix acorn flour fifty/fifty with wheat flour and make any bread or pastry product (even pasta).

Cacti

In general, any palatable cacti can be eaten. This means you must know what is a cactus, and what is not a cactus. There is a *Euphorbia* that closely resembles a prickly pear cactus *(Opuntia);* however, when you cut the *Euphorbia,* it bleeds out a milky sap. Don't eat any *Euphorbias.* Some cacti are too woody to eat. Some are too bitter.

Prickly pear cactus. The glossy green new growth is tasty in salads.

Scraping the small glochids and larger spines from the cactus pads.
DOLORES LYNN NYERGES

Slicing the cleaned cactus pads. DOLORES LYNN NYERGES

And though botanists generally regard the fruit and tender parts of all cacti as being a safe group, Cody Lundin of Arizona reports that several individuals have gotten sick from eating one particular species of prickly pear *(Opuntia)*. Though we've not yet identified the exact species, always exercise caution with any new food until you know your body accepts it.

The author collects ripe prickly pear cactus fruit.
TIMOTHY SNIDER

Fruits and tender parts of cacti, once cleaned of their spines, can be eaten raw, sauteed, or cooked with other vegetables.

Cattails

Cattails are found worldwide in wet areas. These are the tall, grassy plants whose fruit resembles a hotdog on a stick. There are several edible portions on this fellow, from top to bottom. When the flower spike is green in the spring, you can boil them and eat them like corn on the cob. Just above this green spike is the male pollen, which can be shaken into bags to collect. The pollen can be added to bread and pancake batter.

You can also briskly tug up a young shoot in the spring and summer, and peel back the outer green leaves to get the inner white core. Once the plant has produced a flower spike, the shoot will be fibrous, so you need to pull only the young ones. The inner white core has a flavor similar to cucumber and is great in salads and cooked dishes.

The young, tender shoot of a cattail.

The mature cattail flower spike. When young and green, these spikes can be boiled and eaten.

Chickweed

Chickweed is found worldwide in lawns, fields, and hillsides. It is a delicate, weak-stemmed plant with opposite leaves that come to a sharp point. Each flower consists of five petals, each of which has a deep cleft, giving the appearance of ten petals. There is also a barely noticeable line of fine white hairs along one side of the stem.

Chickweed is short-lived, and is generally available only in spring and early summer. Collect chickweed and use it in salads. It is great as the only salad ingredient, and it goes well with other salad ingredients.

Young chickweed.

A flowering dandelion.

Dandelion

Dandelion is found worldwide, typically on lawns and fields. It has the characteristic yellow flower, followed by the "seed-ball" that children love to blow and scatter to the wind. The leaves are deeply incised and are said to resemble a lion's tooth.

The leaves are one of the richest sources of beta-carotene, richer than carrots. Use the leaves in salads (they are bitter) or cooked in greens or vegetable dishes. The roots can also be washed and boiled like parsnips, or they can be made into a caffeine-free coffee substitute. Dry and grind the roots, roast them, and percolate the results as you would coffee grounds.

Sow thistle, a dandelion relative, grows several feet tall. Sow thistle leaves and root can be eaten like dandelion.

Note that the margins of the curly dock leaves are wavy or curly.

Dock

Curly dock is found throughout most of the world in fields, lawns, and wetlands. It is so persistent with its perennial root that it is regarded as a serious agricultural pest. The leaves, rich in vitamin A, are added sparingly in salads or can be added to sautéed dishes or soups.

The root is commonly used in herbal medicine, and goes by the name yellow dock.

Grasses

Grasses are found on every landmass in the world. From grasses, we get leaves and seeds, which are some of the most important cereal crops in history (corn, wheat, rice, barley, sorghum are all grasses).

Curly dock seeds mature to a chocolate brown color.

Young grass leaves can be eaten in salads or cooked in soups. The older they are, the more fibrous they become. The young leaves can also be pressed in a juicer to extract their nutritious juice.

The seeds can be collected and used in cooked cereal dishes or as flour for bread and pastry products. Never use grass seeds that are moldy.

Lamb's-Quarter
Lamb's-quarter can also be referred to as wild spinach, and it is found worldwide. It is one of the richest sources of vitamins and minerals for any plant, wild or cultivated.

Lamb's-quarter.

Use the young leaves in salads, soups, egg dishes—anywhere you'd use spinach. Use the seeds in soups and bread batter.

Mustard

Various members of the Mustard Family are found worldwide. This includes not only the plants we call "mustard," but also such plants as watercress, sweet alyssum, radish, and others. Mustards typically have a sharp or spicy flavor. The young leaves are usually good in salads, and some are best cooked. Most have flowers that can be eaten. Some have harvestable seeds or seedpods that are also delicious.

Members of the Mustard Family are recognized by the fact that their flowers have four petals, six stamens, four sepals, and one pistil.

A young mustard rosette.

Young watercress, a relative of mustard.

Onions

Onions are a group within the Lily Family, typically the *Allium* genus (though there are a few species outside of this genus that are commonly regarded as "onions"). If you have a good sense of smell, you can always recognize an onion by its aroma. If there is no obvious aroma, don't eat the plant since some members of the Lily Family can be poisonous.

Eating any members of the onion group is an easy way to "eat our medicine." Add them to soups, salads, sandwiches, or egg dishes.

Purslane

Purslane is a low-growing plant that is found worldwide. You recognize it by its round and reddish stems, its paddle-shaped leaves, and its yellow flowers. Purslane is the best plant source of omega-3 fatty acids.

The plant, once cleaned, is good in salads, soups, and most cooked dishes. It has a crisp texture and good flavor. Even Thoreau wrote about eating purslane when he was living in his little cabin out on Walden Pond.

The paddle-shaped leaves of purslane.

Musician Jon Sherman looks at Pacific Ocean kelp (seaweed).

Seaweeds

Seaweeds are found in marine waters worldwide. They comprise the macroscopic marine algaes of the brown algae group, red algae group, and the green algae group. Kelp is a very common example of a brown algae.

When you collect seaweeds for food, make sure they are fresh and not beginning to decompose. Also, do not collect seaweeds for food where there is ocean pollution.

There are so many seaweeds that it is hard to generalize. Some are ideal raw; others are best cooked. Some must be dried to be palatable. This is a very nutritious food group; seaweeds are great added to soup stock or powdered and used as a salt substitute.

You can study plants every day of your life, in the city or in the woods; you don't need to wait for a major earthquake or hurricane to do this. If you try to learn which wild plants are edible AFTER the disaster has hit, it will be safer to stick with other conventional forms of food until you gradually learn how to identify what is edible.

OTHER SOURCES OF WILDERNESS FOOD

We have made many delicious and satisfying meals from just plants. But for extended time in the wilderness, plants alone might be insufficient. There was a reason why vegetarianism was nearly unknown by cultures of the past. The balance of nature persists by animals eating others and being eaten. It is largely a brutal existence. Only kill when you must, and eat what you kill! Furthermore, learn to use other parts of the animals besides just the meat such as the bones and hide.

Begin with what is easiest to capture. Most small larvae and insects can be readily captured, cooked, and eaten, but only the somewhat larger ones are worth the effort. We have collected termite larvae in dead trees, and swatted dozens and hundreds of grasshoppers, and cooked them. Despite the fact that I find limited value in the *Survivor* TV show, or *Fear Factor,* they have both amply demonstrated that just about any grub and crawling thing *could* be eaten. However, the best policy is to always cook and to avoid the brightly colored bugs and insects.

A student on a field trip tries on a gopher snakeskin as a headband.

All fish can be eaten. In some cases, they can be captured by hand. Ron Hood of Hoods Woods *(survival.com)* demonstrates how easy this can be done in the right terrain in his excellent video series. Fish can also be taken with simple nets and simple fishing lines. Your challenge will be to make hooks, bait, and line from natural materials.

All birds can be eaten. They can be taken with bolas, throwing sticks, thrown stones, and various ingenious snares and traps.

All snakes and lizards can be eaten. Obviously, you must use extreme caution when capturing a poisonous snake, such as a rattler.

Frogs have a long history of being used for food—you are eating mostly legs with them. Some frogs should be avoided, however, as well as salamanders. Here is a story from a firsthand observer. A student asked a biology teacher whether or not it was true that the skin of a certain frog was toxic. The class was out on a field trip and the teacher just laughed. He picked up the frog and licked its skin. The teacher immediately fainted! We don't know what would have happened had this little creature been eaten

Gary Gonzales shows a simple sling for hunting small game. DUDE McLEAN

A figure-four deadfall for catching small game. DUDE McLEAN

for its scant flesh, but obviously there was some toxicity in that skin. Therefore, as with all "new foods," always exercise appropriate caution.

Rabbits, squirrels, rats, monkeys, possums, and the many "smaller"
animals of the woods and jungles can all be eaten. As usual, the challenge
is to capture them with nets, or blow guns, or arrows—whatever.

Larger game, also, can be used, *if* you have the skills to capture such
animals. Deer, of course, are the most abundant and widespread. But there
are parts of the world where pig are abundant, and various other animals.

SUMMARY OF FOOD IN THE CITY

- *Animals:* Rats, squirrels, possums, pigeons all thrive in urban areas. If you have the ability to capture them for food, you are also ridding the city of possible sources of disease. Cook them well! In a genuine large-scale urban emergency, any domesticated animals will disappear somewhat quickly. If you love your cats and dogs, hide them!
- *Plants:* Wild foods are common in the city. So are edible ornamentals, fruit trees, and gardens. You should always plant useful plants and learn to store some of what you grow. Stored foods can be dried, pickled, frozen (as long as you have electricity), and canned.
- *Miscellaneous:* You *should* have a home food storage and add to it regularly. Buy what you eat and eat what you store! You don't necessarily get the best quality or the best price by buying in bulk. Use manufacturers' coupons and build up your storage that way. Don't buy large cans of food that will require refrigeration upon opening, unless you are with a large group that will use it all up once opened.

In the urban setting, what sort of animals will be available after the major emergency? After a really serious large-scale disaster, the stores will be shut down or looted after a few days. After all the backyard rabbits and chickens are eaten, cats and dogs will be the primary targets. That will be the brutal and gruesome reality of a really serious long-term survival situation. Eventually, people will realize they can eat squirrels, possum, rats, pigeons, snails, lizards, and whatever else they can capture.

On the other hand, by planning ahead, and by making the effort to organize your neighborhood so that everyone is producing something and everyone is able to work together, you can create a neighborhood food source that will allow you to survive a disaster in strength, not in weakness.

There are two aspects of backyard urban food planning. You must *store* and you must *produce*. Let's discuss production first.

FOOD PRODUCTION

Every tree in your yard or garden should be a food producer, appropriate to your region. If not food, it can be a source of medicine, soap, fiber, or some other useful product. The same goes for shrubs and other plants. Do some very basic research and find out what fruit and nut trees, vines, cacti, vegetables, herbs, medicines, fiber plants, and soap plants will grow well in your area. Skip a lawn altogether and landscape your yard with useful plants. This is an enlightened form of self-interest, since you will benefit from this every day, whether or not you are ever faced with a severe emergency.

By the way, from the viewpoint of survival thinking, you may not want to have a landscaped yard that shows *obvious* food production. You might be the first target and casualty after a serious emergency. Plan your trees and shrubs into your yard's landscaping. Grow various food plants in every nook and cranny, without the need for straight rows.

You need to decide specifically what to grow, based on your tastes, and your locale. A lot of the consideration in plant selection can be found in *Extreme Simplicity: Homesteading in the City* by Christopher and Dolores Lynn Nyerges (White River Junction, VT: Chelsea Green Publishing, 2003).

Once you learn about the common edible weeds, you will be doing much less work as a gardener. In fact, I like to say that learning how to eat the edible weeds is a simple way to double the amount of produce from your garden.

Possibilities for urban animal husbandry (for meat, milk, and eggs) include the raising of chickens, ducks, miniature pigs *(great fertilizer),* goats, rabbits, and bees.

The details of raising animals in the backyard or small farm have been well-covered in such books as *Grow It!* by Richard Langer (New York, NY: Avon Books, 1974) and *The Homesteader's Handbook to Raising Small Livestock* by Jerome Belanger (Emmaus, PA: Rodale Press, 1974).

FOOD STORAGE

Food is part of life. If our normal supplies were immediately stopped, it would certainly be a major inconvenience. By itself, a stoppage of normal food supplies to a town or city won't mean that you will die—you just have to look elsewhere until the normal farming supply lines are reestablished.

Besides what you are able to produce on or near your own property, you should store as much as you can for your family. The subject of food storage has been fully delved into in James Talmadge Stevens's book, *Making the Best of Basics.* He explains how much of certain items you should store, where to buy them, and how to prepare them.

In a nutshell, here is what you should consider about food storage.

1. It is not necessary to spend thousands of dollars to buy someone else's "food storage system." In many cases, it is not economical to go that route, and you may end up buying foods you wouldn't normally eat.

2. Follow the old saying, "Store what you eat, and eat what you store." One of the first steps in choosing what to buy for storage is to make a list of what you already like and already eat. Start by buying extra

Gilbert Nyerges and son have some of their "food storage" for breakfast.

Five-gallon plastic buckets store grains and seeds.

Dolores Lynn Nyerges shows boxes of dried food purchased at an estate sale for a fraction of the original cost.

of those items. Then, don't just have food storage in some remote cellar or closet. Use those items you are storing. This means you will be continually rotating your food supplies.

3. Most of your food supplies should not be frozen. Choose dried foods (grains, seeds, noodles, dried fruits, dried vegetables), and canned goods (modern canned goods can last up to ten years, depending on contents. For examples, tomatoes last the least amount of time). Also consider some retort bag foods (e.g., Meals Ready to Eat [MREs] and some backpacking food), that don't require refrigeration.

4. A simple way to get started is to buy double every time you do your regular shopping. If you normally buy four cans of soup for the family, buy eight instead, and so forth.

5. One way to make this as economical as possible is to clip and use manufacturers' coupons for those items you normally eat. Then use those coupons at the stores that double the amount of the coupon.

6. Grains and seeds are excellent to store because they contain lots of energy and they last a long time. But, remember, store what you eat. I know *many* people who stored hundreds of pounds of wheat, which sat in their garages twenty years until they got rid of it. They assumed that they would use wheat if there was ever a major disaster, but eating wheat was not a normal part of their routine. It would have made more sense to buy lima beans, rice, split peas, or some other such food that they actually used regularly.

7

Tools and Weapons

Survival kits, weapons, tools—these all go hand-in-glove with survival. It doesn't matter if you're in town or in the backwoods, a survival kit (even the most minimal one) is *always* needed.

BASIC SURVIVAL KIT

Perhaps the best single reference on making your own survival kit is John McCann's *Build the Perfect Survival Kit* (Iola, WI: KP Books, 2005). Get it, read it, and follow his advice.

Here are my ideas. The most basic survival kit is a knife, fire starter, and some twine. These three items—along with your knowledge and skills—enable you to do most of what is needed in a survival situation.

Back in the late 1970s, I met survival instructor Denny Hughes who was training Boy Scouts in Pasadena. He showed us a "survival necklace" that they sold as a Scout fundraiser. It consisted of a Swiss Army knife (not a knockoff), a Doan magnesium fire starter, and a whistle. It was all on a paracord, so you could wear it around your neck. You could lose your pack, lose your pants, and you'd still have this minisurvival kit. Other than the whistle (which is good, but not essential), I still carry variations of the Denny Hughes survival kit to this day.

If I was preparing for a longer survival situation, I would prepare and have a more extensive kit. What follows is the basic list that I have provided for individuals attending my weekend survival skills classes.

PERSONAL BRING LIST

Clothing:
(*Note:* This is not a complete list, but a list of clothing-related recommendations.)
> One change of clothing (any more would be too bulky)
> Rain protection
> Sun protection (hat, eyeglasses)
> Comfortable shoes, moccasins, or boots
> Hand protection
> Extra shoelaces
> A large bandanna has *many* uses

Sewing Kit:
> Needles
> Various threads (Kevlar thread is virtually tear proof)
> An awl
> Small scissors
> Safety pins

Pack

Compass
(*Note:* A compass aids orienteering.)

Topographical Maps of Area

Note Pad and Pens/Pencils
(*Note:* These are a MUST.)

Water Containers:
Quart-containers (at least two per person)

Water Purification:
> Iodine crystals OR
> A commercial pump filter

Eating Utensils:
(*Note:* Bring no other utensils; learn to make chopsticks, wooden spoons, bowls, etc.)
>   Sierra Cup (or equivalent)
>   Five-pound coffee can with a wire handle

Basic First Aid Kit:
>   A small container of raw honey
>   A container of raw vinegar
>   One leaf from an aloe vera plant
>   Castor oil or other skin moisturizer to deal with chapped lips
>   and hands

Shovel or Digging Tool

Knives:
(*Note:* Pack all three ideally.)
>   Heavy-duty sheath knife
>   Multiblade Swiss Army–type knife (Preferably Victorinox but
>   Leatherman and other comparable multitools also OK)
>   Heavy-duty lockback

Sharpening Device:
>   A stone
>   A steel (*Note:* I carry an Eze-Lap Diamond Knife Sharpener.)

Firearms or Weapons

Fire Starters:
(*Note:* Please, no matches.)
>   Magnifying glass
>   Magnesium fire starter (everyone should have one of these *all*
>   *the time*)

Tinder Box (Waterproof Container):
(*Note:* Also collect special tinders as you hike along.)
    Finest (grade 000 or 0000) steel wool
    Cotton stuffing
    "Fatwood"
    Oiled and waxed sawdust
    Dried mugwort leaves

Whistle

Personal Toiletry Items:
    Small toothbrush
    Small towel
    Toilet paper (don't bother; collect your own)
    Soaps (*only* biodegradable)
    A natural bristle brush (Not just for your hair but for the
        important "dry-washing" of your body when water is
        scarce)

Shelter:
(*Note:* Make it light!)
    Tarp
    Space blanket
    Tube tent

Sleeping Bag
(*Note:* Though I do not always carry a sleeping bag; if you do, I
suggest carrying the lightest one possible.)

Lightweight Cord (about Fifty Feet)
(*Note:* Cord (or twine) has *many* uses. Parachute cord is probably
the best overall; if it's not available, buy a clothesline at the hardware store.)

A Small Flashlight with Extra Batteries
(*Note:* These are not mandatory, but useful.)

The above list, or some variation of it, should be assembled by everyone and kept ready to use in any emergency where your only option is to carry whatever you can.

I don't expect anyone to rotely follow what is written here. I expect you to look at this as one person's result of testing and experimenting, which you should then take into account as you make up the kit that is appropriate to you.

Get John McCann's book, study it, and make your own kit.

Keep in mind that after a disaster, anyone wearing a visible pack is also a target by those who didn't plan accordingly. This is why having a group (family, friends, church, school, business) with which you develop survival strategies is very important. Individuals never fare as well as a cohesive group. Also, the street realities of a post–disaster scenario are why "weapons" are on any good survival list.

Students at International Shootist Institute hone their shooting skills.

WEAPONS

Firearms use and selection is outside the scope of this book—largely because the issue has already been adequately dealt with elsewhere. For starters, read Mel Tappan's *Survival Guns*. Though Mel has long since passed away, and though some of the book is dated, it is still a great primer on what is out there, and why you should consider certain firearms. There is also an excellent section in this book on primitive weapons.

Additionally, become familiar with the National Rifle Association and their magazines, *The American Hunter* and *The American Rifleman*. You receive your choice of magazines when you become an NRA member. Even if you are undecided about firearms, join the NRA at least for a year to get the magazine and get a good, up-to-date introduction to the complex issues regarding firearms.

Dude McLean shoots with a handmade longbow.

SILENT WEAPONS

Weapon	Ability to manufacture in the wild	Ease of Operation	Need of practice
Sling	Since the sling is merely a leather or canvas strap, slings can be easily made if such is available in wilderness.	Relatively easy, once you get the feel of it.	Initial practice is necessary to learn how to swing and release the sling.
Slingshot	Can be made if you have a forked stick and rubber bands (or elastic material such as a piece of clothing).	Any child can quickly master this.	Minimal.
Boladeros	May take a few hours, but can be done if suitable rock, leather, or canvas (to hold rocks) can be found. Argentine Gauchos use rocks, ostrich necks for pouches, and leather twine. Rocks with holes would work well.	Fairly easy. The action is similar to the spinning and releasing of the sling.	Practice needed to be able to spin and release properly so bolas spread (without tangling), and hit its target.
Boomerang	Best would be to buy one at a sporting goods store. A true boom must be well-balanced, flat, and have a proper air foil. In the wild, one can easily make a crude non-returning "rabbit stick."	Relatively easy to use, but must be thrown NOT like a Frisbee, but over-head, vertically, with a snap of the wrist.	Practice required to use this tool for hunting; If unskilled, don't rely on this method for hunting.
Spear	Can be quickly and easily made by fire-hardening a long, straight piece of wood.	Hitting a moving target with a primitive spear can be quite difficult.	Practice, strength, and coordination are all needed to effectively use a spear.

Distance	Urban applications	Cost	Comments
Possibly twice the distance of a slingshot; depends on the user's skill.		Under $5.	Requires skill to be truly effective and accurate; can be deadly in skilled hands.
Most effective under 20 yards.	Can be used to chase away dogs, pigeons, and other small game.	From $1 to $15.	Most effective with small game at short distances; usually stuns rather than kills.
Depends on overall weight and style of bola; generally will travel less than 25 yards.	Immobilizing stray dogs.	Approx. $30.	Can be most effective weapon for bringing down birds and crippling/ensnaring (but not necessarily killing) larger game.
Can be thrown at least 100 yards and return.	Sport and recreation at a local park (but be careful).	From $3 to $25.	Great for skill and coordination development. Skilled Australian Aborigines once used sharpened booms in warfare and to kill game.
Depends on user and quality of spear. Don't expect much accuracy over 25 yards.	Walking stick.		Best restricted to short-range uses, such as fish and frog spear.

SILENT WEAPONS continued

Weapon	Ability to manufacture in the wild	Ease of Operation	Need of practice
Atlatl	There are a variety of styles, but the atlatl is relatively simple to construct.	Acts as an extension of the arm and increases effectiveness of spear.	Much practice is needed in order to hit targets.
Bow	Even a "quickie" bow would take about two days to make properly. Need straight shafts for arrows, fibre material, and some means to fasten feathers to arrow shafts if using feathers.	Depends on bow and person. Crossbows and compounds are far easier to use than home-made or recurves.	Requires at least a year of regular practice to be skillful for hunting big game. Less time for small game. Wilderness-made bows may be inherently ineffective.
Blowgun	For the amateur, best to buy a hollow tube at the hardware store. In the wild, you'd need to hollow out a long straight branch, and you'd have to fabricate darts with available materials.	Amazingly simple. A hard blow through the tube (while aiming) is the procedure.	Practice improves your shot, but very little is needed to use the blowgun effectively.

TOOLS

KNIVES

First, let's start with a knife or a cutting tool.

You should *always* carry some sort of knife with you—*always,* as in "at all times." Though today's knife world is complex with many choices, you should carry at least a folder and a sheath knife as the most basic gear.

If I had to make a single recommendation for the folder, I would suggest a Swiss Army knife (Victorinox is the only genuine Swiss Army knife), with any of the folders from Leatherman or Gerber a close second.

Distance	Urban applications	Cost	Comments
Perhaps doubles the range of a hand-thrown spear.			Increases speed and distance of spear, but the value of this is dependent of skill of user.
Unless you are skilled, under 50 yards is your accuracy range.	If you have the space, practice in your backyard. Has potential as self-defense method where silence is needed.	From $20 (for toys) to several hundred dollars.	A most valuable silent weapon IF you're skilled and have a quality bow. Not a weapon you can just pick up and easily master.
Accuracy recorded up to 100 yards. A Cherokee blowgun has reached distances over 200 yards.	Use to stun stray dogs, coyotes, and even rats. Potential as a self-defense tool, and doubles as a walking stick.	Make yourself for about $5, or pay up to $30.	An ideal all-around survival weapon. Can deliver as much power as a .22; if one is accurate, can kill small game, and larger game with poisoned darts.

There are many other very good folders out there, from Buck to Gerber to Winchester, but I'd still say that the Swiss knife and the Leatherman are your first choice in terms of quality and reasonable price.

For a sheath knife, the choices are vast. I always prefer a carbon steel blade for the sheath knife, with a full tang. The tang is the part of the metal that goes into the handle. Some knives have just a stub of a tang that goes into the handle, which is obviously not as strong as the full tang. The full tang is usually obvious—you can see that the metal is the full size of the handle, with a piece of wood riveted to each side of the tang.

The contents of Doug Haipt's pockets which are mostly knives. At top left is also a fire starter, and to the right, a pair of ratchet clippers.

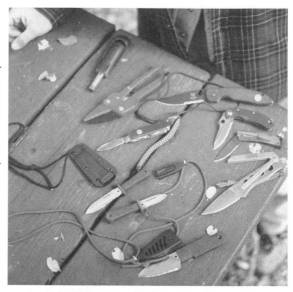

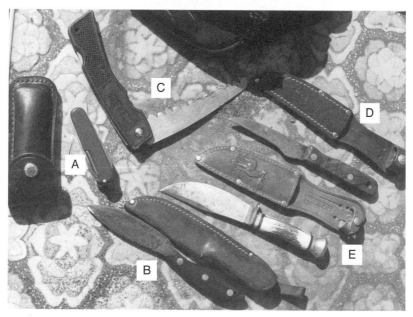

A. A Swiss Army knife.
B. A Grohmann knockoff.
C. A folding saw.

D. An old Herter carbon steel.
E. A German antler-handled sheath knife.

For your money, some of the best knives out there are made by Buck, Gerber, Grohmann, Cold Steel, Tops, Case, and most of the many traditional brands. I particularly like the Cold Steel "Bushman."

There are custom knives out there too, such as the great line by Rik Palm of San Diego *(bladegallery.com)*. As with everything in life, quality takes a little longer and costs a little more, but you're rarely dissatisfied with quality.

What is the ideal length of the sheath knife? This depends on your size and weight, and your intended use. While I have a few wicked beastly knives, most that I carry on a regular basis are smallish blades about three to four inches long. Though I have been occasionally ridiculed by the Rambo crowd (you know, the guys with knives that weigh many pounds and seem to be at least three feet long), I have found that the shorter blade is what I use 90 percent of the time for my all-around camp needs.

From top left: two magnesium fire starters; a Grohmann knockoff; a Herter carbon steel; an Eze-Lap diamond knife sharpener; a Swiss Army knife; (at bottom) a Florian ratchet clipper. The "C"-shaped object is a striker for fire starting. All the above represents a very basic "Survival Kit."

But that's just me. Buy the knife that fits your hand, and feels comfortable to hold. Though a guard is not essential, make sure that you'll have a good grip on the blade so your hands don't slide off the handle and onto the metal if the knife is wet, oily, or bloody.

Whether a folder or sheath, look the knife over for craftsmanship. Do all the seams fit tight? Is everything well polished? Does it walk and talk (referring to a folder that should open smoothly—"walk"—and snap crisply into place—"talk")?

Things *not* to be overly concerned about: if the knife is shiny (this means next to nothing, and the carbon steel blades will take on a dull gray color in time); if the blade is sharp (you can make any metal sharp, but will it hold that edge?); if the knife is attractive (colors or painting on it are irrelevancies).

Here is a simplistic comparison between stainless steel and carbon steel ("simplistic" because some of the advanced steels used by knife makers have blurred the line between "stainless" and "carbon"):

Stainless Steel	Carbon Steel
Generally, it won't rust, so you don't have to be as careful with it.	It will turn gray in time and will rust, so you need to clean and lightly oil blades after use.
Generally, these blades won't hold their edge as well as the carbon steels.	The edge will hold up longer with rugged use than a comparable stainless blade; thus it does not have to be sharpened as often.

Knife Sharpener

If you carry a knife, obtain a knife sharpener and learn how to use it. There are many options available, ranging from steels, ceramic sticks, and oilstones, to more abrasive diamond rods.

My first two choices in sharpening devices are the Eze-Lap diamond knife sharpening rod and a flat bar made from aircraft aluminum—only because I learned how to do sharpening with them.

The many options in sharpening devices have varying degrees of abrasiveness. What's "best" depends on your abilities and preferences. When you buy a sharpening device, *read all the instructions and follow them.* Each device is a little different, so familiarize yourself with the specifics of whatever you choose.

What to Do in a Wilderness Environment When You Didn't Carry a Knife?

Knives and cutting tools can be made from myriad natural and man-made materials. Native Americans without steel made a broad array of cutting tools from what they found in nature and, later, what they managed to trade or scavenge. Look at this overview.

Natural materials	Man-made materials
Bones	Toilet tanks
Obsidian (volcanic glass)	Glass
Antler	Hard plastics
Shell	Various metals
Wood	
Stones (especially, flint, chert, quartzite)	

Knives, awls, digging tools, and so on, are all made from bone, antler, shell, wood and even plastic by simple abrasion. Stones and glass require a bit more skill, such as pecking, grinding, and flint knapping. Though most

A bone abraded into a functional knife-awl.

Scouts who diligently apply themselves can learn these skills in a weekend, the details have been adequately laid out in the biannual issues of *The Bulletin of Primitive Technology* (P.O. Box 905, Rexburg, ID 83440), and such books as John and Jeri McPherson's *"Naked into the Wilderness"*: *Primitive Wilderness Living and Survival Skills,* published by Prairie Wolf, Box 96, Randolph, KS 66554.

OTHER EDGED TOOLS WORTH CONSIDERING
Ratchet Clippers
I consider my ratchet clippers as valuable and useful as my knives. I nearly always carry a pair. The originals were manufactured by the Florian company; these are still available. They are the best quality of what's out there, and the most expensive. There are also numerous knockoffs that are readily available at garden supply stores and hardware stores.

Saw
A hand saw is a critical piece of equipment. I currently carry a Gerber or a Corona folding handsaw. There are several good ones available. Compared with a big heavy knife, a saw makes it fairly easy to remove a piece of wood for a craft project with minimal damage to the tree.

What about wire saws? Don't waste your money on the cheap backpacking wire saws. They are designed for just a few uses, and then they break. If you insist on a wire saw, buy one made from a length of chain saw chain. In catalogs and backpacking stores they sell for around thirty dollars. You can also make your own by buying the chain at a garden supply store, then breaking it apart and adding loops to each end.

Another option is to obtain a medical wire saw used for amputations. Though you may need to search for these a bit, they are as compact as the backpacking wire saw and last a lot longer.

PACKS
Something in which to carry our gear—while this may not be important "surviving" in the backyard at home, it becomes immediately important once you hit the road.

Backpacks, daypacks, fanny packs—these are ubiquitous at discount stores, backpacking stores, yard sales, and sporting goods stores. Have several and keep at least one loaded with a survival kit to just grab if such ever becomes necessary.

You don't want to run down the trail or evacuate the city with important possessions in paper bags. In cases where there is urban unrest, you might not get very far with a pack on your back either, since it makes you a target. Gang members might say, "Hey, there are some supplies on that guy's back that I could use." In some cases, a pack would therefore be useless and you'd need to carry whatever gear you were able in an inconspicuous way—in vest pockets, pants pockets, around your neck, strapped to your leg, in an inconspicuous fanny pack, etc.

So you didn't plan ahead? Here are some pack and container ideas.

Pants Pack

This is one of the easiest makeshift packs. It is easiest done with pants. First, tie off the legs, then fill the pant legs with things you need to carry—

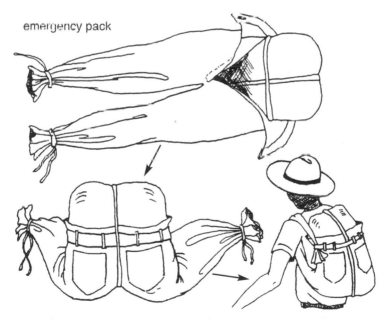

emergency pack

Pants pack. With just a small amount of twine, you can transform an ordinary pair of pants into a functional pack. You can also do the same with a long-sleeved shirt.

Tying up pants into a pack (while Popoki plays with the cord). DOLORES
LYNN NYERGES

ideally soft things, since the pant legs will be your pack straps. Then fill the
rest of the pants with your gear. Use a belt or cord to tie up the waist, and
tie the end of each pant leg to the waist. That's it! You can adjust the straps
as needed, but otherwise you're ready to go.

You can also use a long sleeve sweat shirt for this. Even a button-up
shirt will work, though there are a lot more holes where you might lose
small things.

A Pack from an Old Blanket

This is another simple design for a small pack. Follow the pattern here and
cut it out from an old blanket, drapes, or even thin carpeting. Obviously,
you'll need your sewing gear—scissors, needles, thread.

Decorative packs and shopping bags are made like this, and if made
from good fabric, they are very durable.

As a variation, make the straps longer so the pack can be carried over
one shoulder rather than on the back.

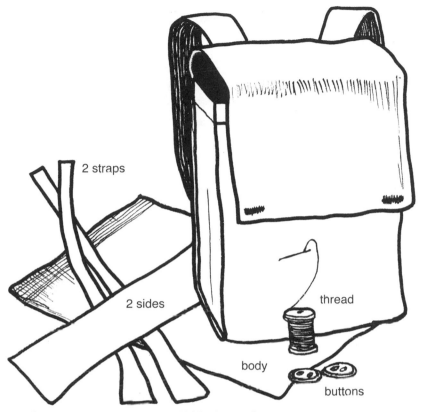

A simple pack made from an old blanket or drape.

CONTAINERS

Agave and Yucca Containers

Agave and yucca plants grow throughout the entire western half of the United States, and in other parts of the world as well.

My first exposure to one of these quiverlike containers was a night in Temple City, California, when I was teaching a survival skills course at Harley Swiftdeer's dojo. After the class, Harley brought me a quiver with some weapons to look at but the container interested me more than the weapons in it! The container came from Africa, Harley said, and by the vascular bundles on the outside, it was clearly a relative of either agave or yucca. That it was such an *obvious* use for a very common material in the wild fascinated me.

Gathering agave and yucca flowering stalks after they died and dried, I've hollowed them out. Some I burned out, which seemed more trouble than it was worth. These stalks were easiest hollowed out with a knife and a straightened-out metal clothes hanger. Once most of the soft pithy inside was gone, I continued to work the inside with a long stick to get it as clean as possible.

There are many possible ways to add a strap to such a container, depending on your available supplies and how you intend to carry it. Most of my carrying straps were very simple. I'd drill two small holes into one side of the tubular container—one toward the top and one closer to the bottom. Then, I took a suitable length of leather cord and tied a large knot on one end. Running the cord through the hole closest to the bottom, from the inside, I pulled it out. The knot kept the cord in place. Putting the cord into the upper hole from the outside, I tied another knot from the inside.

Sizing up a dead yucca flower stalk.
DUDE McLEAN

Cutting a length of the dead yucca flower stalk. DUDE McLEAN

Two finished quivers (the one on the left is made from agave, the right one from yucca), and one long piece of yucca. RAUL CASTELLANO

This secured the cord to the agave container; the strap was done. Finally, I tied a piece of leather to the bottom. (Any other suitable material would work for a bottom.)

When I teach others how to make such a container during some of our field trips, a few guys always wonder if they can avoid having to make a bottom by simply hollowing out the agave (or yucca) stalk from one end. Yes, it can be done, but it takes so much longer to hollow out the tube. If you only intend to use such a container for arrows, then this works fine since you can stick your arrows, points down, into the thick fibrous material of the inner agave stalk. For general purposes, however, hollow the stalks out from both ends and then add a bottom.

BIRCH BARK DESIGN

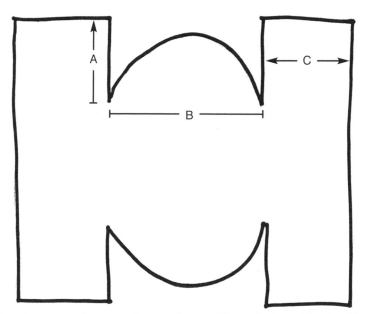

Here is a general pattern that can be used for a birch bark basket. Note the length of each side (A) must be longer than at least half the length of the basket (B). The height of the basket is determined by the length of C. Holes can be burned into the birch bark at even intervals with a hot needle and then sewn up. The birch bark is made pliable by soaking in water. Note: You can use this pattern with other materials also.

The author holds a birch bark container he made. On the ground is birch bark and three birch bark knife sheaths.

DUDE McLEAN

Birch Bark Design

If you live in an area where you can obtain birch bark, here is a simple design for making a bowl or even a pack. To do this well, you will need a knife, and probably scissors, thread, and a needle.

Remember to also use the bark from fallen birch trees; it "keeps" for a long time after it has fallen.

Fold-a-Cup, Big or Small

Perhaps you need a container for eating or carrying small things. A very simple fold-a-cup can be made with paper, cardboard, or even fabrics. To make one of these, you should be able to use just a knife or scissors.

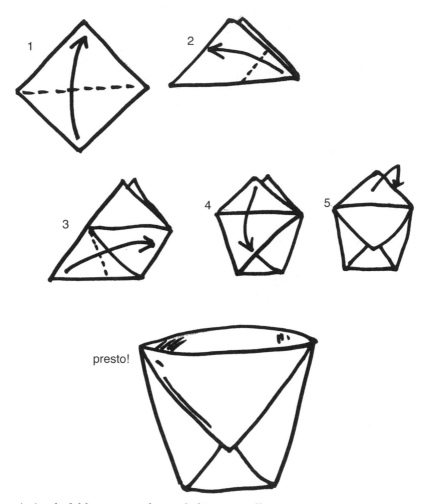

A simple fold-a-cup can be made big or small.

African Man's Bag

Here's a simple bag design that I first saw in the pages of *Wilderness Way* magazine. It was described as a man's bag from a certain tribe in Africa.

Its beauty is in its simplicity: one piece of leather, sewn up by the sides. There is no top flap, just one piece of leather folded in half with a slit for entry.

I use bags like this on the trail for collecting mugwort leaves for tinder—"you can never have enough mugwort"—and for other trail needs.

At some of our weaving classes, students make one of these from old canvas or pants fabric, or leather (rawhide or tanned). Each student first makes a pattern from paper, traces the pattern onto the fabric or leather, and then cuts it out. After the sides are sewn up, the carrying strap can be made of shoestrings, parachute cord, or leather.

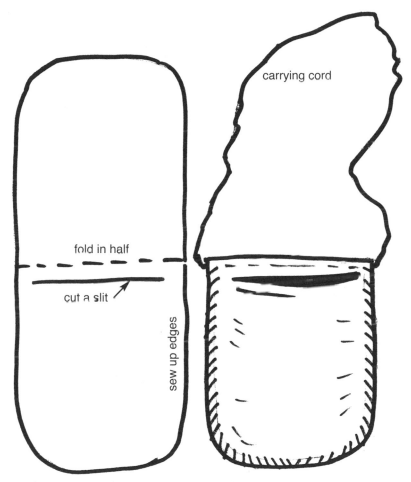

An African "man's bag." Pattern on left; finished bag on right.

*An African
"man's bag."*

Simple Round Pouch

This is a simple carrying device for tobacco, seeds, coins, or other small items. It can probably be made large enough to carry something the volume of a basketball, but this design seems to be best for smaller loads.

Begin by cutting a round piece of fabric or leather. The simplest form of this pouch involves gathering the edges up and tying it with a cord. Or, punch holes around the edge, and string it with a cord. This secures the cord to the pouch and allows you to have a way to open the pouch only as much as needed.

The World Is Full of Containers

When you're on the road and on the move, you obviously need something in which to carry your gear. If you haven't taken the time to purchase a fine pack or other container, remember that nature provides well. Take the time now to learn nature's secrets as well as the skills to avail yourself of those "secrets."

Besides the raw materials for containers already mentioned, wood, clay, and gourds have been used for millenia.

A large piece of wood with a burl to be made into a bowl. DOLORES LYNN NYERGES

The author with a large piece of wood ready to be carved into a bowl. In the foreground is an oak burl cup and an alder burl bowl. DOLORES LYNN NYERGES

Wood can be used for packs, bowls, cups, canoes, and dozens (if not hundreds) of other possibilities. In the photos, see the large wooden slab that I carved and burned into a salad bowl. Look for the desired shape in wood first, then just carve away everything that doesn't look like a salad bowl, a cup, or whatever it is that you "see" in the wood. Note the oak cup and alder bowl in the foreground, both made by burning and carving a burl.

Working with clay does not provide a "quickie" container, but clay has provided generations of people with all the bowls, cups, and cookware they needed. Locate the clay, clean it of all foreign matter, and then make your pots and bowls. After it dries thoroughly, fire it in any of the variations of

A selection of
"pinch pots" being
prepared for firing.
DUDE McLEAN

Cody Lundin inspects a gourd that will be made into a water container.
DUDE McLEAN

the primitive kilns. The details of pottery making have been widely published in such journals as the *Bulletin of Primitive Technology* and such books as *Earth Knack: Stone Age Skills for the Twenty-first Century* by Bart and Robin Blankenship (Layton, Utah: Gibbs Smith, 1996). Additionally, nearly every ceramics teacher in every high school and college can tell you about how to make pots and bowls "from scratch." Use your local resources!

Gourds likewise have been used for millennia as water containers, bowls, cups, scoops, and more. Perhaps the easiest way to introduce yourself to the art of gourd craft is to purchase several hard-shelled gourds from a farmers' market, and simply experiment with making large spoons, cups, and bowls. Though this has been widely discussed in craft and survival books, one of my favorite references is Ellsworth Jaeger's *Nature Crafts* (New York: Macmillan Publishing Co., 1949).

In the photo, survival instructor Cody Lundin is conducting a workshop in making water containers from gourds at the annual Winter Count event in Arizona.

8

First Aid

This book does not focus upon emergency first aid. We strongly urge you to sign up for a Red Cross emergency first aid course, held year-round at cities around the country. The Red Cross also has an emergency first aid textbook, which you should obtain, read, and study.

Here are a few basic guidelines to keep in mind with emergency first aid situations. Cuts, scratches, abrasions, and burns are by far the most common circumstances requiring medical attention.

Nevertheless, according to the Red Cross, shock can be the major hazard in any accident. Thus, once you've treated the victim for his/her wound (burn, broken bone, cuts), you should always treat for shock.

SYMPTOMS OF SHOCK

Here are the signs of shock:

General weakness

Hallucinations

Pale, cool, and clammy skin

Weak, but rapid pulse

Confusion and disorientation

Shock accompanies all major and many minor physical accidents.

TREATING FOR SHOCK

To treat shock:

1. Have the victim lie flat
2. Cover the victim to prevent heat loss, even on a warm day
   a. It is better, however, for the victim to be slightly cool than too warm.

In all cases where there is bleeding, especially profuse bleeding, do whatever it takes to stop the victim's bleeding, and then treat for shock.

More serious medical emergencies (strokes, heart attacks, broken bones, and so on) require experienced medical attention. Though the body has a remarkable ability to heal itself, we should still do everything we can to facilitate that self-healing. Take the Red Cross emergency first aid course and learn all you can about first aid and healing. Consider then the following guidelines in that larger context.

This simple outline of natural first aid for survival situations summarizes some of the common household items that can be used to treat illnesses.

Honey

(*Note:* Research has shown that raw, unheated honey is most effective for medical use.)

A. Effective as an antiseptic (arrests or prevents the growth of micro-organisms):
  1. Apply directly to wounds
  2. Effective due to hygroscopic properties, i.e., it deprives bacteria of their needed moisture
B. Use only *raw* honey to treat:
  1. burns
  2. open wounds
  3. blisters
  4. abrasions
  5. punctures
C. Carry it regularly and use it (sweetening coffee for instance) so it is always handy

Lemon

(*Note:* Its effectiveness is due to its citric acid.)

A. Acts as an astringent to draw out toxins
B. Also acts as an antiseptic (although less effective than honey)
C. Can also be used to make refreshing drinks; lemon is the best drink to consume in heat and stressful situations
D. Juice can be used to treat dog bites

Vinegar
(*Note:* It must be raw apple cider vinegar, which contains a living culture.)
  A. Similar properties to lemon; also has astringent and antiseptic
     properties
  B. Ideal to consume one tablespoon vinegar per quart of water during
     hot weather
  C. Consuming vinegar helps to repel fleas and mosquitoes
  D. Countless other "medicinal" uses—see *Folk Medicine* by Dr. DC
     Jarvis
  Also see The Vinegar of Four Thieves, page 233

Garlic and Other Onion Family Members
(*Note:* Garlic contains a powerful antibacterial agent, allicin.)
  A. Can be mashed and applied externally to wounds to prevent
     infection
  B. Can be eaten with food
  C. When eaten, acts as a chelator, which helps to remove lead and
     mercury from the body and protects the body from the effects of the
     same

Vitamin C
  A. Increase dosage during periods of high stress

Vitamin E
  A. Can be used externally to condition the skin
  B. Should be taken in excess during any heart-related stresses

Aloe Vera
  A. Best when used fresh; the "processed" aloe is a distant second-best
  B. Ideal treatment for fire burns
  C. Good way to treat any skin cuts or bruises
  D. Ideal for sunburn
  E. The best treatment for poison oak rash

Eric Zammit shows his backyard aloe vera plant.

Velia Rivera shows a poison oak leaf (she is immune to the toxic oil).

Food Poisoning
A. In some cases, best to induce vomiting
B. Three "old-fashioned" remedies for food poisoning:
   1. Black "burnt" toast (for the carbon)
   2. Black tea (for the tannic acid)
   3. Milk of magnesia (to coat the stomach)

Emergency "Penicillin"
In the "old days," moldy bread was sometimes applied directly to a wound. Depending on the type of wound and actual molds on the bread, this can be risky.

Lessons From Hiroshima
Based on a study of the dietary habits of Hiroshima survivors, three foods were identified as being extremely valuable to protect the body from harmful effects of radiation:
   1. Seaweeds
   2. Wheat grass (and/or wheat sprouts)
   3. Soy tofu

THE VINEGAR OF FOUR THIEVES
An attention-grabbing story appeared in a past issue of the *Forest Voice*, newsletter of the Forest Preservation Society of Southern California, edited by Karin James.

It seems that some centuries ago during an outbreak of bubonic plague in France, four thieves managed to loot empty plague-ridden homes without contracting the dreaded plague. Arrested by policemen, these four thieves were brought before the French judge in Marseilles. Wondering aloud, the judge asked how it was possible that these four thieves managed to resist the plague, especially since they had been in and out of so many plague-infested homes.

"We drink and wash with this vinegar preparation every few hours," they answered. The judge made a shrewd bargain. The thieves would be given their freedom in exchange for their "anti-plague recipe."

This recipe is recorded in Dian Buchman's *Herbal Medicine* book. Buchman writes, "this recipe has been used for centuries, but legend has it that it was discovered during a devastating bubonic plague." Here's the recipe, which was printed in the *Forest Voice* and reprinted in our *Talking Leafs Newsletter:*

Vinegar of Four Thieves

2 quarts (half gallon)	2 T rue
apple cider vinegar	2 T rosemary
2 T lavender	2 T wormwood
2 T sage	2 T mint

Combine the herbs and steep in vinegar in the sun for two weeks. Strain. Add 2 T of garlic buds and steep for several days. Remove. To preserve, add 4 oz. of glycerin.

According to Karin James, the vinegar recipe can be used for washing floors, walls, windows, and will offset smells in the home. It helps to deter bugs if you rinse your hiking gear in it. She also saves the herbs when she strains them out of the vinegar and places them where ants come into the kitchen. "It works," she states. "No more ants!"

So why would this simple herbal remedy help with plague? Much has been written about the antibiotic properties of garlic, as well as the health benefits of raw apple cider vinegar. In fact, books have been written just about these two ingredients. We suspect that these are the most important parts of this old remedy.

Please note that the above commentary on first aid pertained primarily to physical injuries. Here is something else to consider.

It is not only the physical accidents that we need to be concerned about, whether in a wilderness accident or as the result of an urban disaster (major earthquake, flood). In studies that have been done of the survivors of major disasters, the following conclusions have been made about their mental state. Approximately 15 percent made quick, appropriate, and efficient choices and performed actions that were well-suited to their safety and security. Another 15 percent "went crazy," making wild irrational choices and even getting hurt as a result of their "losing it." The rest, about 70 percent of the survivors—a full majority—neither went crazy nor did they make wise and efficient choices and actions, but rather wandered about somewhat zombielike, spaced-out, in a state of stupor and shock, simply not knowing what to do, where to go, what to think. This shocked majority tends to be passive, but will take orders from someone who seems to be in control and who seems to know what he or she is doing and why.

The point: None of us wants to be a part of that majority, and definitely we don't want to be a part of that "crazy 15." What can we do to ensure that in a time of disaster, we find ourselves with the 15 percent who perform wise, appropriate, efficient actions?

None of us really *knows* what we will do until we are actually tested in difficult, stressful real life conditions. It is impossible to predict what you might do when you are seated comfortably in your home drinking a warm beverage. The only way to expand our mental and physical limits is to actually put ourselves into situations where we can discover more about ourselves during situations of less sleep, less food, more work. People in the military often get that experience. Some survival schools offer these experiences. And anyone (with a group of friends and supporters) can regularly plan such trips with the express purpose of safely expanding limits, learning how to react in times of stress, and attempting to make the right choices when it is not easy to do so.

9

Navigation

NOTE: This book does not comprehensively deal with navigation and direction-finding. Though an important—even critical—topic, it has already been addressed fully in other forums. We will only share a few basics here.

For an introduction to the map and compass, purchase a copy of *Be Expert with Map and Compass* by Bjorn Kjellstrom (Hoboken, NJ: Wiley, 1994). Also get of copy of *The Green Beret's Compass Course* by Don Paul (Path Finder, Box 500, Kalaheo, Kauai, HI 96741). Don Paul's method for keeping track of your travels with only a compass and a notepad is one that I regularly teach and recommend.

Also, for making sun compasses, and learning star navigation and other natural signs, get a copy of Ron Hood's *NAVIGATION* video (volume 4 of his Woodsmaster series) from *survival.com.*

A MAP

A map of your terrain is always more important than the compass, assuming you have to choose between one and the other. The map is an aerial picture of your terrain, location of roads, buildings, water, towns—everything you need to know. The topographical map is the map of choice because it gives you a visual depiction of the rise and fall of the land. This enables you to choose the easiest route (which is not necessarily the shortest) between two points.

A COMPASS

A compass certainly makes the map more useful, since it enables you to accurately align the map with the actual terrain. When you buy a

Students learn how to use a map and compass at an orienteering class.
DUDE McLEAN

compass, *read all the instructions* that come with it, and practice all the exercises that the manufactures provides.

With only a compass, you can accurately travel in a straight line for miles through fog or forest, and then go back the same way you came.

Besides the references already listed, one of the best ways to learn to use a map with a compass is to enroll in a junior college class on orienteering or participate in a few programs with a local orienteering club.

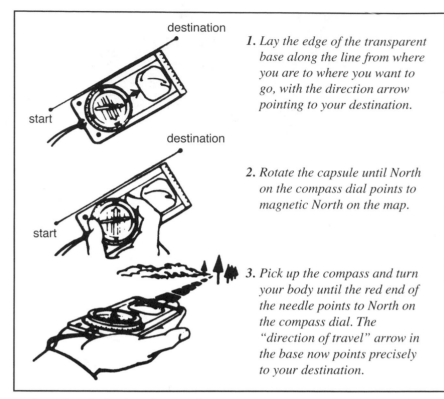

destination

1. Lay the edge of the transparent base along the line from where you are to where you want to go, with the direction arrow pointing to your destination.

start

destination

2. Rotate the capsule until North on the compass dial points to magnetic North on the map.

start

3. Pick up the compass and turn your body until the red end of the needle points to North on the compass dial. The "direction of travel" arrow in the base now points precisely to your destination.

Learning the basics of map and compass use.

STARS

The North Star is *not* the brightest star in the sky. If you follow it with time-lapse photography, the North Star appears to be stationary, and all the stars appear to rotate counterclockwise around it. If you were standing on the north pole, the North Star would be directly overhead. Time-lapse photography is capturing the rotation of the earth.

To find the North Star, locate the Big Dipper. The North Star is in a direct line with the two end stars of the Big Dipper (see illustration on page 240).

Go outside on a moonless night and get to know the constellations. Begin with the Big Dipper and Cassiopeia. Get to know Orion.

Once while driving in an unfamiliar part of Los Angeles with a friend, we got hopelessly lost. I was able to stick my head out the window, see the Big Dipper, and determine in which direction we should drive to get to our destination. It worked!

THE GREAT CLOCKFACE OF THE STARS
Telling Time by the Stars

Sundials have been made and used with great efficiency for thousands of years. But did you know that you can also tell time at night by the position of the stars?

In the Northern Hemisphere, all the observable stars appear to rotate in a regular counterclockwise motion around the North Star. A given star, observed through a fixed site, will return to the exact site of the first observation in 23 hours, 56 minutes, and 4.09 seconds. This period of time—known as the "sidereal day"—nearly corresponds to our standard day of 24 hours.

Telling time by the stars necessitates knowledge of the following:

1. You must be able to accurately identify the constellations of Cassiopeia and the Big Dipper, and be able to locate the North Star; and
2. You must then be able to "read" the position of the stars and make a few adjustments to translate sidereal time into your local standard time.

First, Let's Learn How to Identify the Constellations

Go outside and face the north on a clear night. A place as free as possible from obstructions along the northern horizon. Stars will be difficult to observe during the full moon and near the bright lights of the city.

Now, referring to the accompanying illustration, look for the easily recognized Big Dipper. Three stars compose the "handle" and four more stars compose the roughly rectangular "bowl" of the dipper. Do you see it?

The Big Dipper (Ursa Major, Big Bear) and Cassiopeia are on opposite sides of Polaris.

The two end stars of the Big Dipper serve as pointers to find Polaris.

You must be able to locate Beta Cassiopeiae, a star in the constellation Cassiopeia, in order to use the Star Clock.

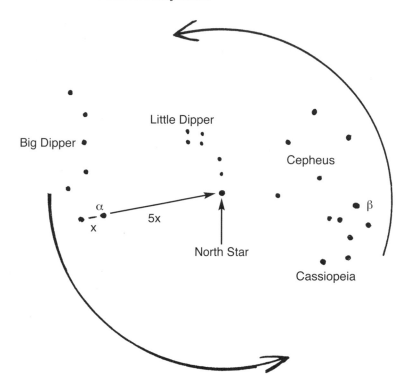

The North Star (Polaris) is the apparent center of the northern circumpolar constellations. In the Northern Hemisphere, all stars appear to rotate counterclockwise around Polaris.

Cassiopeia appears like an "M" or a "W."

Do not confuse Cepheus with Cassiopeia. Cepheus appears as a square with a triangle on the top; the tip of the triangle points near Polaris.

The two outermost stars of the "bowl" point directly at the North Star. If we designate the distance between the two pointer stars as x, then the north star is found at the apparent distance of 5x from the Big Dipper.

Did you locate the North Star? It is *not* the brightest star in the sky, as erroneously believed.

Keep in mind that the North Star is the pivot point around which all the stars appear to rotate counterclockwise.

On the side of the North Star opposite the Big Dipper, we find Cassiopeia's Chair, or Cassiopeia. Depending on the time of night, Cassiopeia is said to look like an "M," a "W," or a chair. It is important to have a clear picture of the relationship between Cassiopeia and the Big Dipper.

Cassiopeia is located approximately 180 degrees from the Big Dipper, with both constellations traveling in the same (more or less) concentric ring around the North Star.

We know that the two pointer stars of the Big Dipper and the North Star lie on a line. If this line is extended beyond the North Star, one of the stars of Cassiopeia comes close to the line. This star, Beta Cassiopeiae, misses the line by about 15 degrees.

Once you're able to locate these constellations, you'll be able to utilize them for ascertaining the time at night.

Now you are ready to use the star dial provided in this book. Photocopy the star dial – you may want to enlarge it when you are copying it, since you want it at least seven inches wide for ease of operation. Then mount it on heavy cardboard. Cut out the center hole. At the points marked "A" and "B," punch holes with a pin. Attach a cord to those holes. The cord's end should extend beyond the bottom edge of the dial. Attach a nut or some other object to the end of the cord to serve as a plumb line.

Now you're ready.

On a clear night, hold the dial with the numerals facing you so that the North Star (Polaris) can be seen in the center of the hole. Turn the dial so that the plumb line lies along the line from the central hole to the numeral 12.

Now, hold your star dial at such a distance so that Beta Cassiopeiae appears just on the edge of the dial. Make sure the North Star remains in the middle hole of your dial. Now read the position of Beta Cassiopeiae, approximating as closely as possible the fraction of the hour. This reading is the hour angle of Beta Cassiopeiae, also termed the local sidereal time.

Now we can convert the sidereal time into our standard time.

At around March 21 each year, the sun is at the vernal equinox and its right ascension is zero hours. (Right Ascension corresponds roughly to the longitude lines on the earth's surface, and it is measured in hours, minutes, and seconds.) The daily average change in the right ascension is just about four minutes per day or two hours per month.

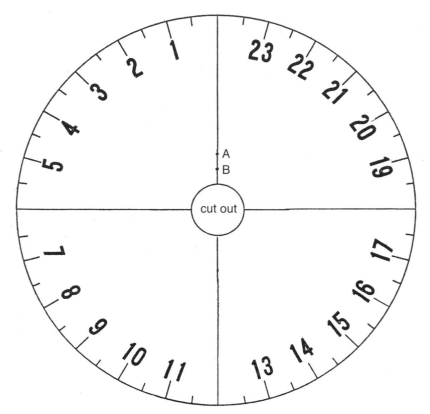

Telling Time by the Stars with the Star Dial.
1. *S.T. – R.A. = H.A.*
2. *H.A. + 12 = L.C.T.*
3. If East: *L.C.T. – Corr. = Std. T.*
   If West: *L.C.T. + Corr. = Std. T.*
4. If DST: *Std. T. – 1 hr. = DST.*

Therefore, the right ascension is most easily figured by adding four minutes per day for each day that has elapsed between March 21 and the date of your observation. Subtract the right ascension from the observed sidereal time. This gives you the hour angle of the mean sun; thus, *Sidereal Time – Right Ascension = Hour Angle.*

Next, you must add 12 in order to obtain the local civil time—this is because the hour angle tells us how many hours have elapsed since noon, but civil time is reckoned from midnight: *Hour Angle + 12 = Local Civil Time.*

Next, you need to correct for the longitude from where you are observing in order to obtain standard time. To make this correction, you first need to know two things:

1. The precise longitude of your observation; and
2. The precise longitude of the standard for your time zone.

The first is obtained by checking a topographical map of your area or by calling a map shop or local geologist.

The second is also simple; refer to the chart below:

Time Zone	Standard
Pacific	120° W
Mountain	105° W
Central	90° W
Eastern	75° W
Atlantic	60° W

Timothy Snider shows how to align the Star Dial.

To obtain your longitude correction, you need to figure the difference between your time zone standard and your point of observation. Since each degree represents four minutes of time, you multiply your difference by four. This gives you your correction.

If you are observing east of your time standard meridian, you must *subtract* the correction from the local civil time. If you are observing west of your time standard, you must *add* the correction to the local civil time.

Here are the formulas:

> *East:* Local Civil Time − Correction = Standard Time
>
> *West:* Local Civil Time + Correction = Standard Time

Since most of your observations will likely be made at one location, you'll not need to refigure this last one over and over again.

Finally, you subtract one hour if you are currently operating under daylight saving time.

That's it!

If each concept described here has been clearly understood, you now should be able to accurately obtain the correct time from the stars. Though a reference book on basic astronomy will provide you with a fuller description of these concepts, everything you need in order to determine time from the stars is provided here.

It may happen that you cannot see Beta Cassiopeiae. In such case, you can use Alpha Ursae Majoris (a star in the Big Dipper) as your reference star. In this case, the sidereal time will be the reading on your dial plus eleven hours.

At times when I couldn't see Beta Cassiopeiae, I've fairly accurately estimated its position. By observing Alpha Ursae Majoris, I was able to determine—with near accuracy—the position of where I *knew* Beta Cassiopeiae *had* to be.

The following summary is for your ready reference:

> *Step 1:* Sidereal Time − Right Ascension = Hour Angle
>
> *Step 2:* Hour Angle + 12 = Local Civil Time
>
> *Step 3: East:* Local Civil Time − Correction = Standard Time
>
>   *West:* Local Civil Time + Correction = Standard Time
>
> *Step 4: (If Daylight Saving Time):*
>
>   Standard Time − 1 hour = Daylight Saving Time

An example will clarify all of the foregoing points. I am at home in northeastern Los Angeles. The date is June 21. I go outdoors, locate the North Star, and I position my star dial so that the North Star is in the dial's middle hole. I make certain that the dial is properly aligned so that 24 is at the top and 12 at the bottom. Next, I locate Beta Cassiopeiae and position the star dial so that Beta Cassiopeiae is observed just at the edge of the dial. I observe Beta Cassiopeiae at 17½ on the dial. I can now put the star dial away and do some figuring.

First, I figure the right ascension. June 21 is exactly three months from the vernal equinox (March 21), so the right ascension is easily figured: At two hours per month, the right ascension equals six hours. I subtract 6 from the 17½ reading and I get 11½.

Now I add 12 and I get 23½, or 11:30 P.M.

As stated earlier, the standard meridian for the Pacific Time Zone is the 120th meridian. I live at 118° 12', which is east of the standard. The difference between 120° and 118° 12' is 1° 48'. Since each degree corresponds to four minutes of time, I multiply this difference by four, which equals 7 minutes and 12 seconds.

As indicated in Step 3, this correction is subtracted from the local civil time. Thus, 11:30 P.M. minus 7 minutes 12 seconds give us roughly 11:23 P.M.

Finally, I subtract another hour since daylight saving time is in use on the date of my observation. The time then is 10:23 P.M.

I look at my watch and I see that I'm six minutes off. Where did I go wrong? When I get home, I check the time and learn that my watch was three minutes off, leaving me with an observational error of three minutes. That's not bad!

With a bit of practice, you'll be able to figure time this way in about a minute or so.

TELLING TIME BY THE SUN

PEBBLE METHOD
There is a simple method to generally tell directions (and time) with a stick and some pebbles. Place a stick into the ground. Put a pebble at the end of the shadow. Wait twenty minutes or so. The shadow will have

moved, so put another pebble at the end of the shadow. Wait another twenty minutes and do this again.

In general, when you are in the Northern Hemisphere, your shadow will be pointing north if the stick is stuck vertically into the ground. (In fact, this is not always so, such as during midsummer when the sun is north of the celestial equator . . . but, read on.)

The shadow's movement, marked by the pebbles, will be eastward, because the sun is moving westward. The shadow should be the shortest around noon, when the sun is directly overhead (directly overhead at 1 P.M. if there is daylight saving time).

If you draw a straight line from the stick to the stone marking the shortest shadow, you should have a north-south line, more or less. A perpendicular line gives you an east-west line and your crude compass.

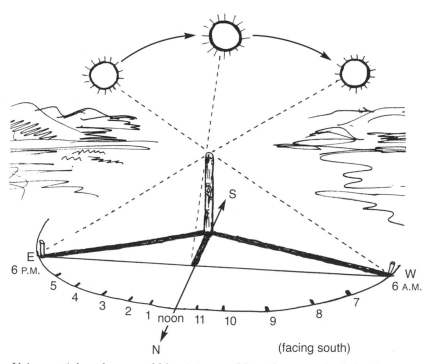

Using a stick and some pebbles, it is possible to figure out both the time and directions.

If you know the approximate time that the sun is rising and setting, you can evenly divide the arc formed by the stones and create a crude but usable sun dial clock.

HOW MUCH TIME BEFORE SUNSET

This is an old way to tell approximately how long it will be until the sun sets. Face the horizon and extend your arm. Tuck in your thumb. Bend your hand so that your fingers are parallel to the horizon. Now, using your four fingers, measure up from the horizon to the sun. Each finger represents about fifteen minutes of the sun's travel across the sky.

This will give you a good idea when the sun hits the horizon. Keep in mind that in the summer, there will still be usable light for at least an hour after sundown. In the winter, things will get pretty dark after the sun dips below the horizon.

If you need to make camp before dark, this is a good way to determine how much light is left.

NATURAL OBSERVATIONS

You have no map, no compass, and you're lost or confused. Are there signs in nature to tell you directions?

We have long heard that moss only grows on the north side of trees. Wrong! Moss grows on the north side, the east side, the south side, and the west side of trees, especially in a dense forest where there is little light. Though there is logic to this idea, and though in a clearing the moss is predominantly on the northern half of the tree (there's less light there), it is not a precise, nor reliable, method of direction finding.

All rivers flow to civilization. This myth has been repeated so often that it seems to be a fact in the minds of many. And since it *sometimes* does work, its efficacy seems enforced. But it simply isn't always so. Just look at a map.

If you are lost, following a stream downstream might lead you into very rugged wilderness. This is not a surefire way to get "unlost."

In fact, there is no single natural observation that will tell you directions. You need to be observant of many features, and collectively — in conjunction with your common sense and "thinking on your feet" — you stand a good chance of determining compass points. Here are a few of those general guidelines—though some would put these observations into the category of "folklore." This is because they are *general* guidelines. Rely on these alone and you may still remain hopelessly lost.

TREES

Tips of certain trees will tend to point in specific directions. For example, the tops of willows, poplars, and alders often point south because they grow typically in canyons or streams, which are (more often than not) flowing southward. But a stream can have lots of bends and curves, so this is only a very general observation that can help in conjunction with other observations.

The tips of pines and hemlocks often point east. These trees are typically found at higher elevations and the tips are affected by prevailing winds. The operative word here is "often," not "always."

BIRDS

It has been said that the holes of woodpeckers are always on the east sides of the trees. This is demonstrably false. In general, however, the pileated woodpeckers tend to peck primarily on the east sides of trees. This is a bit too imprecise to be of any practical value; plus, how many of us can differentiate between the pileated woodpecker and any other woodpecker's holes?

FACING THE SUN

Flowers often face the sun. This is where sunflowers (and the Sunflower Family as a whole) got its name. You can point a time-lapse camera at a sunflower and watch it move throughout the day to face the sun as the sun moves across the sky.

Certain spiderwebs nearly always face the southern direction.

Keep in mind that "facing south" in these cases refers to anywhere from the south-east to the south-west, nearly a full 180 degrees of the horizon.

Any hill or mountain range that runs in an east-west direction will receive the most vegetation on the north side. The south side—exposed more to the sun—will have different plant communities and generally be drier. The north side will retain snow longer and will have more shade, and thus more ferns, moss, and so on. This means that if you had to travel and be quiet, it would be best to walk on the northern side of the hill where there is more moisture. On the south side, there would be drier soil and dry twigs that would make more noise as you walked through.

10

What Is Survival?

OUR CHOICES: ETHICAL, MORAL, SPIRITUAL DECISIONS AND HOW THEY AFFECT OUR SURVIVAL

We have talked about the basics of individual physical survival—water, fire, food, shelter, and so on. These are the basics of individual physical survival.

But there is still *so much* more to survival than merely keeping the body alive. If you do not attend to your health, the very survival of your body is threatened. Likewise, the full scope of survival include mental and emotional survival, economic survival, moral and spiritual survival, and obviously the survival of our families, neighborhoods, countries, and the ecological survival of nature.

A STRATEGY

Our goal should be to avoid in the first place all those situations that can threaten our survival. For example, in wilderness survival situations, the overwhelming majority of life-threatening cases could have been prevented or severely limited if the victims had done one (or all) of the following:

1. Prepared a proper survival kit for the terrain and time of year
2. Made a plan and itinerary of their travels and *shared* it with someone
3. Changed their plans if facing unforseen obstacles; too many bulled ahead stubbornly with their plans when things were going wrong—despite all logic

4. Went with a friend; didn't travel alone

Though most wilderness travelers take the above for granted, why is it that the great masses of people living in the cities do not do this? Shouldn't we have an individual "survival plan" for our lives? Aren't the above four basic survival strategies applicable to our daily life?

Take Action with Your Family

One of the best ways to begin to rectify this situation and render yourself, your family, your friends, your neighborhood less vulnerable, is to have regular work meetings, field trips, or gatherings where you do a combination of educating yourself about the nature of world (and local) conditions, and do some actual hands-on learning of at least one new skill each time you meet.

Your hands-on sessions can include some form of planting and harvesting crops, canning food, drying food, purifying water, learning to make fire with primitive methods, building a quick shelter for your family in the backyard, making your own clothes, weaving baskets and rope, studying codes or a new language, making simple auto repairs, sharpening knives, practicing with firearms, and so on.

If you jump in and start learning from whatever your skill level, your process of learning and doing will make you less vulnerable. Your physical skills will increase and your mental awareness will be sharpened.

Making a Plan

We all need some sort of home "survival kit." You probably already have all the elements, here and there. And we all need some sort of plan (not just a plan on paper!) for our specific situation. If you live in earthquake country, you need an earthquake plan. If you live in the Great Basin, you need a drought plan. If you live under a dam, you need an escape plan. Discuss your plan with family and close friends. Take the time to practice some aspects of the plan.

PERSONAL CHARACTER AND SURVIVAL

Does anyone doubt that the quality of our inner character is directly related to our survivability? It should be obvious that such universal tenets as The Ten Commandments were unquestionably designed for *our very survival!* Giving in to any of the "Seven Deadly Sins" (covetousness, pride, lust, anger, gluttony, envy, and sloth) lessens our survival potential, either by weakening us physically or compromising us mentally and emotionally.

Certainly everyone sees the ultimate enlightened survival value of what has become known as The Golden Rule—do unto others as you would have them do unto you. How can you go wrong with such a simple concept?

THE PYRAMID OF SUCCESS

Famous USC basketball coach John Wooden—called the "greatest coach of all time"—often said that he wasn't training students to be good basketball players, but training them for life. Over the years, he developed a teaching tool that he calls the Pyramid of Success. Obviously, the principles in his pyramid can apply to everyone. Using the pyramid's qualities as a reference is a way to improve our survival quotient.

John Wooden points out that the foundation blocks of his plan are friendship, loyalty, and cooperation. He adds that the heart of the pyramid is skill. "You must be able to DO and DO quickly," says Wooden.

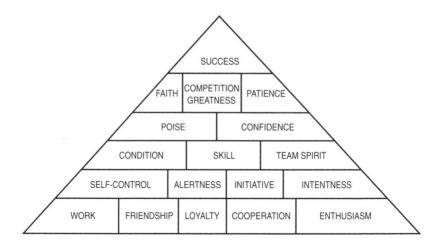

John Wooden's Pyramid of Success

THE SIX PILLARS OF CHARACTER

The Josephson Institute of Ethics is also very concerned about personal character as it relates to the survivability of the individual and the country. These ethicists provide the "Six Pillars of Character" from which all our choices should arise: trustworthiness, respect, responsibility, fairness, caring, and citizenship. All six of these values are needed to improve our character and the quality of our lives. (See their discussion of each of the six on their website at *josephsoninstitute.org*.)

ECONOMIC SURVIVAL

It would be the height of naïveté to discuss the full picture of survival and not bring up money. Money is an integral, inescapable part of life in any specialized and organized society.

This book does not focus upon economic survival issues. If you feel you are lacking in this area, research the areas of investing, real estate, tax laws, appreciation, and insurance, and so on. There is no shortage of solid material that is available—quite the contrary.

Therefore, while I am not intending to provide you with any sort of comprehensive economic advice here, my comments may help to put "money" in a meaningful context. Knowledge and self-education are perhaps the most important first step to increasing your survival awareness and allowing yourself the possibility of making new choices. This concept was the subject of the last chapter of our book, *Extreme Simplicity: Homesteading in the City*.

GOALS

Begin by defining your goals very specifically. Write them down. Record some short-term goals, but also your long-term goals. These must be goals that you deeply desire to achieve, and they should be goals that you *can* achieve. For each goal, you should be able to record at least three concrete steps that you can take—whatever your current financial situation—to achieve these goals.

Also, consider the broadest ramifications for your goals. Are they benefiting more than just yourself? Are these goals that might encourage friends, family, neighbors to work together (thus increasing our survival quotient)?

In *Beautiful Mind,* the movie about the life of John Nash, the mathematician who developed "game theory," Nash quotes Adam Smith (often referred to as the father of modern economics) as saying, "The best result comes when everyone in the group is doing what's best for themselves." In other words, self-interest should serve the group. Certainly we can say that *enlightened* self-interest serves more than just the individual. But Nash saw that Adam Smith, while correct, was incomplete. Nash enhanced Adam Smith's axiom to: "The best result comes when everyone in the group is doing what's best for themselves—**AND the group.**"

It was clear to a mathematician that when you only care about yourself, and do not bother thinking about the concerns of others, that you are thereby *NOT* going to achieve the maximum best results for yourself or the group. In other words, basing your actions upon how they will positively affect others IS a way to get the best for YOU. Thinking about others is definitely in your best "survival" interests.

Principles

Here are some financial-related principles to ponder and to experiment with. Think of them as tools for survival.

1. "As ye give, so shall ye receive."
2. Always lead with an offer. (Don't expect someone to care about you just because you are in need. Before you ask for help, find out how you can benefit the other person.)
3. Make every place better for your having been there. (This is true appreciation.)
4. What blesses one, blesses all. (Another way of saying "all ships rise in a rising tide.")
5. Discover the magic of tithing. (Even financial advisor Suze Orman suggests that you give to the church or charity of your choice.)
6. Pay back your debts, both financial and nonfinancial.
7. Barter and exchange. (You'd be amazed at the sorts of relationships that can develop when money is *not* involved.)

ENVIRONMENTAL SURVIVAL

HOW WE AFFECT OUR ENVIRONMENT
(LOCALLY, CITY-WIDE, NATIONALLY, INTERNATIONALLY)

Our actions upon the environment have a profound effect upon our survival. Earthquakes, floods, tsunamis, fires, droughts, ice ages, high winds, volcanic eruptions have been with us since the beginning of memory and will continue to be with us. Although we cannot stop the forces of nature, we must begin to see how our actions (and inactions) absolutely exacerbate the effects of these natural forces and definitely affect our ability to survive.

Drought

Take drought, for example. Do human actions have any effect on drought conditions? Absolutely! Some have attempted to prove that the great drought of the 1930s and the resultant Dust Bowl era were the result of poor farming practices. In order to maximize farming areas and to farm with the greatest of convenience, trees were cut down and the soil was not properly fertilized.

The land had no life and the dry winds blew the barren top soil away.

Fires follow drought, and there have always been natural fires that moved through certain areas. It is known by biologists that certain ecosystems require fire. When we settle an area and believe we have conquered it, we no longer allow the fire to cleanse the land; the stage is set for horrific fires that cannot be stopped.

Rain

Heavy rains are common after the drought and fire cycle is played out. Such rains often do result in flooding and landslides. The effects can be lesser or greater, however, depending upon what we have done to the land. In some cases, houses should never have been built on steep hillsides, since the building of the houses requires cutting down the trees and reshaping the terrain. With the trees gone and much of the land paved over, the water must go somewhere when it rains. The trees and the soil can process a fair amount of the water, but with trees gone and no way for water to percolate into the soil, the water flows downhill, creating disasters for those who live in the mud's path.

Earthquakes

A major earthquake could occur at any time along any of the major fault-lines throughout the world. Although we cannot stop the shaking, we can realize that we live in such an area and plan to minimize the impact upon our family's life in the aftermath, such as improving our building standards, storing water, organizing friends, having knowledge of first aid, and so on.

And some earthquakes may indeed have been caused by the hand of man. There are some scientists who believe that the Long Beach, California, earthquake of 1930 was the direct result of overpumping oil from the underground reservoirs there.

It would be difficult to plan for some disasters—like a large comet hitting your neighborhood. Assuming you survived, so much would be devastated that "waiting for help" would not be a viable option. If you valued life you would have developed skills that now would be useful in the postapocalyptic world. (To read a possible scenario of a large comet hitting the earth, read *Lucifer's Hammer* [by Larry Niven and Jerry Pournelle, 1977].)

Tsunami

A major tsunami occurs in the aftermath of an earthquake, and there may or may not be warning given to the people of the potentially affected area. With a few hours warning, you'd have time to grab your prepared survival pack, don the running shoes that you always keep by the door, and flee to higher ground. Once again, not much survives a thirty-foot wave traveling at over fifty miles per hour; there are no building codes anywhere in the world that are designed to deal with such worst-case scenarios. So your key to survival is awareness, preparedness, and in knowing how to quickly think on your feet. In the days following a tsunami when all semblance of your town has been destroyed, you'll want to make a fire, purify water, find a toilet spot, and organize with other survivors.

Plague

Plague is by no means extinct on the earth. Various communicable diseases (both those known and unknown) can travel throughout the world quickly, due to air travel and places where large numbers of people gather (malls, sporting events).

People living in a relatively small area and poor sanitation exacerbate the spread of disease. In fact, in most natural disasters, health officials often point out that there are more deaths from hepatitis A, dysentery, and so forth (caused by the poor sanitation following the disaster), than were directly caused by the disaster itself. Knowing how to purify water in very primitive conditions and knowing how to set up a safe and sanitary toilet are two skills that can literally mean the difference between life and death.

(By the way, for some literary adventures into a world stricken with a mysterious plague, read both *The Wall* by Marlen Haushofer [originally published in Germany] and *Earth Abides* [by George R. Stewart, 1949]. Put yourself into the position of the main character(s) and ask yourself, "What would I do if faced with a similar situation?")

Last but not least is overpopulation. It is a simple fact that any given area can sustain a somewhat finite number of people utilizing the resources from that given area. Of course, we have been able to break this law of nature for so long because we find ways to take water from other areas and we also trade for food and oil that come from elsewhere. This is something that will ultimately affect most people in the world.

CULTURAL SURVIVAL

According to archaeologist Joseph Tainter, author of *The Collapse of Complex Societies*, there are eight definable reasons why civilizations fall.

1. Resource Depletion
2. New Resources
3. Catastrophes
4. Insufficient Response to Circumstances
5. Other Complex Societies
6. Intruders
7. Mismanagement
8. Economic Explanations

Examples of Tainter's observations are found each day in the daily newspapers. Survival is not an academic, intellectual idea. This is the reason we have all endeavored to learn and to practice everyday survival skills.

DARK AGES AHEAD?

According to social critic Jane Jacobs, author of *Dark Age Ahead,* we are following the same cultural decline that occurred with the Roman Empire. She begins her book by telling us that dark ages are a lot more common than we may think, and she identifies many of the weak spots in our contemporary lifestyle.

Her list of weak areas includes: taxes, family, community, education, science, technology, the lack of self-policing, and moral/ethical insanity.

Jacobs believes that these weak areas are the foundation of all the other often-cited problems, such as the environment, crime, and the discrepancy between rich and poor.

Jacobs points out that modern families are "rigged to fail" due to rising housing prices, the suburban sprawl (with a reduced sense of community), and the automobile. She believes the automobile is the chief destroyer not only of communities but of the *idea* of community.

The hopeful part is that Jacobs does not see dark ages as inevitable. For one thing, we all need to get involved and be a part of the solution. Jacobs points out that the millions of details of a complex, living culture are not transmitted via writing or pictorially, but by (1) living examples and (2) by word of mouth. Jacobs goes on to say that though "the end" may be near, there are things we can do. What are those actions?

We need to think.

We need to model solutions.

We need to teach, to lecture, and to write.

The stereotypical survivalist who hides out in a cave or cabin with his beans and shotgun is the antithesis of survival. He is not engaged in society in any meaningful way and is therefore not a part of any meaningful solution.

SOME "MUST READ" BOOKS

Language in Thought and Action by S. I. Hayakawa.

This is the *the* book for "how to think." If you've not read *and studied it,* get it today from a used book store.

The Art of Loving by Eric Fromme

In the classic book on the problems facing all of humanity, Fromme describes the science of love. This book teaches you "how to love."

True Believer by Eric Hoffer
The quintessential book on mass movements and cults teaches you "how to believe."

Man and Woman and Child by Harold Percival.
This is perhaps *the* most important book on who and what we are, and what is our ultimate destiny.

Democracy Is Self-Government by H. W. Percival.
A "must-read" if you are to grasp what's wrong with modern politics. The author demonstrates that individual Self-government is the only path to real democracy.

FOR FURTHER INFORMATION
Christopher Nyerges and his associates have been conducting field trips, seminars, and classes since 1974. Over 30,000 people have attended these workshops on wild food identification, survival skills (urban and wilderness), energy self-reliance, and more. To learn more about the schedule of ongoing events, as well as the books by Christopher Nyerges, write to the School of Self-reliance, Box 41834, Eagle Rock, CA 90041, or check the following two Web sites: *www.ChristopherNyerges.com* and *www.self-reliance.net.*

Index